Master AZ-104: Be the Azure Admin Employers Want

Kameron Hussain and Frahaan Hussain

Published by Sonar Publishing, 2025.

MASTER AZ-104: BE THE AZURE ADMIN EMPLOYERS WANT

First edition. May 26, 2025.

ISBN: 979-8231116690

Written by Kameron Hussain and Frahaan Hussain.

Master AZ-104: Be the Azure Admin Employers Want

First Edition

Preface

In an era where cloud computing defines the backbone of modern IT infrastructure, Microsoft Azure has emerged as a cornerstone platform for organizations transitioning into the cloud. With growing demand for scalable, secure, and cost-effective computing solutions, businesses across industries are embracing Azure to host applications, manage services, and deliver value. As a result, the role of the Azure Administrator has become not just relevant, but essential.

This book—**Master AZ-104: Be the Azure Admin Employers Want**—has been meticulously crafted to prepare you for the Microsoft Certified: Azure Administrator Associate certification (exam code AZ-104). It also serves as a comprehensive guide for individuals seeking to deepen their practical understanding of managing and maintaining Azure environments.

Organized into nine chapters, the book begins with a foundational understanding of Azure, then dives into identity and governance, storage solutions, compute resources, networking, monitoring strategies, and cost management. These topics directly reflect the AZ-104 exam objectives and align closely with real-world administrative responsibilities.

Chapter 7 is dedicated to preparing for the certification exam with a focus on exam strategy, pitfalls to avoid, and techniques for maximizing your score. Following that, Chapter 8 shifts focus beyond certification, guiding you through real-world scenarios, career progression, and continued professional development. Finally, Chapter 9 offers appendices that include sample projects, a glossary, and frequently asked questions—ideal for quick reference and deeper exploration.

This is the first edition of this book and aims to blend exam-focused preparation with applied knowledge. Whether you're new to cloud administration or transitioning from another cloud platform, this book is designed to build both competence and confidence.

Let's embark on this journey together—not just to pass the exam, but to thrive as an Azure Administrator.

Table of Contents

B

C

D

E

F

G

H

I

J

K

L

M

N

O

P

Q

R

S

T

U

Real-World Operations

Career and Learning

Miscellaneous

Summary

Chapter 1: Introduction to Microsoft Azure and the AZ-104 Exam

What Is Microsoft Azure?

MICROSOFT AZURE IS a comprehensive cloud computing platform created by Microsoft for building, deploying, and managing services and applications through Microsoft-managed data centers. It provides a wide range of cloud services, including compute, analytics, storage, networking, and more. Organizations use Azure to develop new applications or run existing applications in the cloud.

At its core, Azure supports three core cloud computing models: **Infrastructure as a Service (IaaS)**, **Platform as a Service (PaaS)**, and **Software as a Service (SaaS)**. These models offer varying levels of control, flexibility, and management depending on user needs.

Azure's infrastructure spans across over 60 regions worldwide, making it one of the largest public cloud platforms available. These regions are grouped into geographies and are built with availability zones that ensure redundancy and high availability.

Key Features of Azure

AZURE DISTINGUISHES itself with features such as:

- **Scalability**: Resources can be automatically scaled up or down depending on demand.
- **Security**: With built-in tools like Azure Security Center, Key Vault, and Sentinel, it enforces enterprise-grade security.

- **Hybrid Capability**: Services like Azure Arc and Azure Stack allow on-premises and multi-cloud environments to integrate seamlessly.

- **Compliance**: Azure supports over 100 compliance certifications including GDPR, HIPAA, ISO, and FedRAMP.

- **Global Reach**: Azure's data centers are strategically located to meet data residency requirements and optimize performance.

Azure Services Overview

AZURE OFFERS A VAST array of services categorized broadly as follows:

- **Compute**: Virtual Machines, Azure App Services, Azure Kubernetes Service (AKS)

- **Networking**: Virtual Networks, Load Balancers, VPN Gateways, Azure Front Door

- **Storage**: Blob Storage, Disk Storage, File Shares, Data Lake

- **Databases**: SQL Database, Cosmos DB, MySQL, PostgreSQL

- **AI and Machine Learning**: Azure Cognitive Services, Azure Machine Learning

- **Security**: Azure AD, Key Vault, Defender for Cloud

- **Monitoring**: Azure Monitor, Application Insights, Log Analytics

Use Cases for Azure

AZURE IS USED IN A wide range of industries and scenarios:

- **Enterprise IT**: Running internal applications, identity management, backups
- **Web Applications**: Hosting APIs, static websites, scalable app environments
- **DevOps**: CI/CD pipelines, container orchestration, infrastructure automation
- **AI/ML Workloads**: Training models, running inference in real time
- **IoT Deployments**: Ingesting telemetry from edge devices, processing data centrally

Understanding the Cloud Model

AZURE SUPPORTS MULTIPLE service delivery models:

- **IaaS (Infrastructure as a Service)**: Offers virtualized hardware resources like VMs, networks, and storage.
- **PaaS (Platform as a Service)**: Provides managed platforms for developers to build applications without handling infrastructure.

- **SaaS (Software as a Service)**: Delivers software applications over the internet, like Microsoft 365 or Dynamics 365.

Model	Responsibility	Example Services
IaaS	User manages OS, middleware, runtime	Azure Virtual Machines, Virtual Networks
PaaS	User manages only apps and data	Azure App Services, Azure SQL Database
SaaS	Provider manages everything	Microsoft 365, Dynamics 365

Getting Started with Azure

TO START USING AZURE, users need an Azure account and access to the **Azure Portal**—a web-based interface to manage resources. Developers can also interact with Azure via:

- **Azure CLI**: Command-line tool for managing resources.

- **Azure PowerShell**: Module for Windows PowerShell and PowerShell Core.

- **Azure SDKs**: SDKs for multiple programming languages like .NET, Java, Python, and JavaScript.

Sample Azure CLI usage:

Create a resource group

az group create—name dev-rg—location uksouth

Create a storage account

```
az storage account create—name mystorageacct \

—resource-group dev-rg \

—location uksouth \

—sku Standard_LRS
```

Azure Resource Manager (ARM)

AZURE RESOURCES ARE managed through **Azure Resource Manager**, which provides a management layer that enables you to create, update, and delete resources in your Azure account.

ARM templates, written in JSON or Bicep, allow declarative management of infrastructure. Here's a simple example of an ARM template for a storage account:

```
{

"$schema": "https://schema.management.azure.com/schemas/2019-04-01/deploymentTemplate.json#",

"contentVersion": "1.0.0.0",

"resources": [

{

"type": "Microsoft.Storage/storageAccounts",

"apiVersion": "2022-09-01",

"name": "mystorageacct",

"location": "uksouth",

"sku": {
```

```
"name": "Standard_LRS"
},
"kind": "StorageV2",
"properties": {}
}
]
}
```

Azure Regions and Availability

AZURE RESOURCES ARE deployed in regions which represent a set of data centers deployed within a specific geographical location. Key terms include:

- **Region**: Physical location with multiple data centers.
- **Availability Zone**: Physically separate zones within a region to increase redundancy.
- **Region Pairing**: Ensures disaster recovery and failover capabilities.

Example region pairs:

- UK South ↔ UK West
- East US ↔ West US

Pricing and Cost Management

AZURE USES A PAY-AS-you-go pricing model. Tools such as the Azure Pricing Calculator and Azure Cost Management help forecast and control expenses.

Example pricing model for a standard VM (UK South):

Resource	Cost Estimate
B2s VM	~£0.02/hour
128 GB Storage	~£3/month
Outbound Data	~£0.05/GB

Users can also set budgets, alerts, and tags to track usage and control costs.

Azure for Developers and Admins

WHILE AZURE IS DEVELOPER-friendly, it also empowers IT administrators with capabilities like:

- Setting up Active Directory and RBAC
- Implementing automation using Azure Automation or Logic Apps
- Managing hybrid infrastructure with Azure Arc

Admins use tools such as:

- **Azure Portal** (GUI)
- **Azure CLI / PowerShell** (Command Line)
- **Azure Mobile App** (On-the-go management)

Summary

MICROSOFT AZURE REPRESENTS a massive opportunity for professionals across domains. From running virtual machines to deploying global apps at scale, Azure supports innovation, automation, and resilience. Understanding what Azure is and the foundational services it offers is the first step toward becoming a certified and effective Azure Administrator. The next sections will dive deeper into each major area covered by the AZ-104 exam.

The Role of an Azure Administrator

THE AZURE ADMINISTRATOR is a critical role in any organization that leverages Microsoft Azure for its cloud computing needs. This professional is responsible for implementing, monitoring, and maintaining Microsoft Azure solutions, including major services related to compute, storage, network, and security. As cloud adoption becomes the norm rather than the exception, Azure Administrators are at the center of operations, ensuring that the cloud environment remains functional, secure, scalable, and cost-effective.

Key Responsibilities of an Azure Administrator

AN AZURE ADMINISTRATOR'S responsibilities span multiple domains. The following outlines core areas they handle:

- **Provisioning Azure Resources**: Creating and managing virtual machines, web apps, storage accounts, databases, and containers.

- **Managing Azure Identity and Access**: Configuring Azure Active Directory (Azure AD), implementing

Role-Based Access Control (RBAC), and enforcing security principles like least privilege.

- **Monitoring and Optimizing Performance**: Using tools like Azure Monitor, Log Analytics, and Application Insights to track system health and optimize resources.

- **Implementing and Maintaining Networks**: Designing and managing virtual networks (VNets), subnets, VPNs, gateways, and Network Security Groups (NSGs).

- **Automating Workloads**: Leveraging scripts, ARM templates, Bicep, and services like Azure Automation or Logic Apps to deploy and manage infrastructure as code (IaC).

- **Ensuring Compliance and Backup**: Configuring backup and disaster recovery plans with Azure Backup and Recovery Services Vaults, while ensuring compliance standards are met.

- **Cost Governance and Budgeting**: Monitoring usage, creating budgets, and optimizing resources to avoid over-provisioning or unexpected billing.

Real-World Tasks and Scenarios

TO ILLUSTRATE THE SCOPE of an Azure Administrator's work, consider the following scenarios:

Scenario 1: Deploying a Web Application

AN ADMINISTRATOR IS tasked with deploying a .NET web application with high availability. They would:

Create a Resource Group:

az group create—name prod-app-rg—location westeurope

1.

Provision an App Service Plan and Web App:

az appservice plan create—name prod-plan—resource-group prod-app-rg—sku P1V2—is-linux

az webapp create—resource-group prod-app-rg—plan prod-plan—name prodwebapp01—runtime "DOTNET|6.0"

1.

Configure monitoring using Application Insights:

az monitor app-insights component create \

—app prod-insights \

—location westeurope \

—resource-group prod-app-rg \

—application-type web

1.

Scenario 2: Enforcing Security via NSGs and RBAC

AN ADMINISTRATOR NEEDS to restrict traffic to a virtual machine:

Create an NSG to allow only SSH from a specific IP:

```
az network nsg rule create \

—resource-group prod-app-rg \

—nsg-name vm-nsg \

—name allow-ssh \

—protocol Tcp \

—direction Inbound \

—source-address-prefixes 203.0.113.25 \

—destination-port-ranges 22 \

—access Allow \

—priority 100
```

•

Apply RBAC to ensure only the DevOps team can manage VMs:

```
az role assignment create \

—assignee "<devops-group-object-id>" \

—role "Virtual Machine Contributor" \

—scope "/subscriptions/<sub-id>/resourceGroups/prod-app-rg"
```

•

These tasks demonstrate how Azure Administrators balance technical capability, security, and governance.

Core Competencies Required

A PROFICIENT AZURE Administrator is expected to develop and maintain mastery across a wide range of domains:

Area	Core Competencies
Compute	VM management, scaling sets, containers, app services
Identity and Access	Azure AD, RBAC, Conditional Access, Identity Protection
Storage	Blob, File Shares, Disks, encryption, replication
Networking	VNets, DNS, NSGs, Load Balancers, ExpressRoute
Monitoring	Azure Monitor, Application Insights, Log Analytics
Security and Compliance	Azure Security Center, Key Vault, Defender for Cloud, compliance configuration
Automation	ARM, Bicep, Azure CLI, PowerShell, Logic Apps
Cost Management	Budgets, pricing calculator, cost analysis, reserved instances

These are not optional skills—they are foundational to the responsibilities carried by administrators.

Tools Used by Azure Administrators

AZURE ADMINISTRATORS must be adept with a range of tools and interfaces. Some of the most commonly used include:

- **Azure Portal**: The GUI for creating and managing resources.
- **Azure CLI**: Command-line interface ideal for automation and scripting.

- **PowerShell**: Widely used in enterprises for managing infrastructure at scale.

- **Azure Resource Manager (ARM) Templates**: Declarative JSON-based templates for resource deployment.

- **Bicep**: A newer, simpler language for ARM template creation.

- **Azure Monitor**: Comprehensive platform for observability.

- **Cost Management + Billing**: Portal for budget alerts, recommendations, and forecast reports.

Example Bicep file for provisioning a storage account:

```
resource storageAccount 'Microsoft.Storage/storageAccounts@2022-09-01' = {

name: 'examplestorageacct'

location: 'westeurope'

sku: {

name: 'Standard_LRS'

}

kind: 'StorageV2'

properties: {}

}
```

Collaborative Role within Organizations

AZURE ADMINISTRATORS do not work in isolation. They collaborate with:

- **Developers**: To deploy code and ensure infrastructure meets application requirements.
- **Security Teams**: To maintain compliance, monitor threats, and enforce security standards.
- **Networking Teams**: To coordinate on hybrid environments, VPNs, and interconnectivity.
- **Management and Finance**: To stay within budget, forecast costs, and report usage.

They often function as the liaison between cloud engineering and other stakeholders—both technical and non-technical.

Azure Administrator vs Other Roles

WHILE OVERLAPPING AT times, it is important to differentiate the Azure Administrator from related roles:

Role	Key Focus
Azure Administrator	Day-to-day management of Azure resources
Azure Architect	Designing high-level solutions and governance models
Azure Developer	Building and deploying cloud-native applications
DevOps Engineer	CI/CD, automation, infrastructure as code
Security Engineer	Risk analysis, security posture, access control

An administrator may wear multiple hats in smaller teams or startups but must still retain a strong foundation in platform management.

Career Relevance and Demand

AS ORGANIZATIONS ACCELERATE their digital transformation, Azure Administrator roles continue to see high demand. According to Microsoft and job market trends:

- Azure Administrator is one of the top job titles associated with cloud growth.
- Professionals with AZ-104 certification often command higher salaries.
- The role is often a stepping stone toward higher-level positions such as Cloud Architect or Site Reliability Engineer.

Professionals in this role can expect to:

- Manage multi-region deployments
- Secure and monitor mission-critical applications
- Optimize and automate infrastructure
- Provide support and troubleshooting for operational issues
- Stay current with Azure innovations and adapt infrastructure accordingly

Best Practices for Success

- **Document Everything**: Use tags, naming conventions, and change logs to ensure traceability.
- **Apply the Principle of Least Privilege**: Always assign the minimum required access.
- **Use Automation**: Avoid manual tasks when infrastructure-as-code solutions are available.
- **Monitor Continuously**: Alerts and dashboards should be in place from day one.
- **Train Continuously**: Azure evolves fast—commit to ongoing education and certifications.

Summary

THE AZURE ADMINISTRATOR plays a vital role in managing, securing, and optimizing Azure environments. Their scope is broad and impactful, covering identity, network, storage, compute, and monitoring. With responsibilities touching nearly every area of the cloud platform, they serve as the operational backbone for businesses running on Azure. By mastering this role, you not only ensure the reliability and security of your organization's cloud infrastructure but also set a strong foundation for a successful career in cloud computing.

Overview of the AZ-104 Exam Objectives

THE AZ-104: MICROSOFT Azure Administrator certification exam is a role-based certification designed to validate the technical skills and knowledge required for managing Azure cloud services.

It is targeted toward IT professionals who are responsible for the day-to-day management, implementation, and monitoring of Azure environments. Passing this exam proves your ability to administer Azure resources in a secure, efficient, and cost-effective manner.

Purpose of the AZ-104 Exam

THE AZ-104 CERTIFICATION is part of the Microsoft Certified: Azure Administrator Associate credential. It evaluates a candidate's capability to:

- Manage Azure identities and governance
- Implement and manage storage
- Deploy and manage Azure compute resources
- Configure and manage virtual networks
- Monitor and back up Azure resources

The certification is recognized globally and is an essential step for those pursuing roles such as Cloud Administrator, System Administrator, Azure Engineer, or aspiring Azure Architects.

Exam Structure and Format

THE AZ-104 EXAM INCLUDES a variety of question types to assess both theoretical understanding and practical application:

- **Multiple-choice questions**
- **Drag-and-drop scenarios**
- **Case studies**

- **Hot area questions (interactive UI-based selections)**
- **Command-line simulation questions**

Key details:

- **Exam Code**: AZ-104
- **Duration**: Approximately 120 minutes
- **Number of Questions**: Typically between 40–60
- **Passing Score**: 700 out of 1000
- **Cost**: Around $165 USD (varies by region)
- **Delivery**: Pearson VUE (Online proctored or testing center)

You will receive immediate pass/fail notification after submitting the exam and a full score report shortly after.

Skills Measured: Objective Domains

THE AZ-104 EXAM BLUEPRINT is divided into five main functional areas, or "skills measured." Below is an outline of these domains along with the associated weightings:

Domain	**Weight** (%)
Manage Azure identities and governance	15–20%
Implement and manage storage	15–20%
Deploy and manage Azure compute resources	20–25%
Configure and manage virtual networking	20–25%
Monitor and back up Azure resources	10–15%

Let's explore each domain in more detail.

1. Manage Azure Identities and Governance (15–20%)

THIS DOMAIN FOCUSES on identity, access, and governance principles using tools like Azure Active Directory (Azure AD), RBAC, and Azure Policy.

Key Objectives:

- Manage Azure AD users and groups
- Manage subscriptions and governance (management groups, tags)
- Implement RBAC and access reviews
- Create and manage Azure policies and Blueprints
- Implement resource locks and naming standards

EXAMPLE: CREATING A user in Azure AD using Azure CLI

```
az ad user create—display-name "Jane Doe" \
—user-principal-name jane.doe@yourtenant.onmicrosoft.com \
—password "P@ssw0rd123!"—force-change-password-next-login true
```

2. Implement and Manage Storage (15–20%)

THIS SECTION ASSESSES your knowledge of managing storage accounts, data redundancy, access configurations, and performance tuning.

Key Objectives:

- Create and configure storage accounts
- Configure blob lifecycle management
- Secure data using Shared Access Signatures (SAS) and Azure AD
- Implement Azure Files and Azure File Sync
- Monitor and troubleshoot storage

EXAMPLE: SETTING LIFECYCLE policy to move blobs to cool tier

```
{
"rules": [
{
"name": "moveToCool",
"enabled": true,
"type": "Lifecycle",
"definition": {
"actions": {
"baseBlob": {
"tierToCool": {
"daysAfterModificationGreaterThan": 30
```

```
}
}
},
"filters": {
"blobTypes": [ "blockBlob" ],
"prefixMatch": [ "logs/" ]
}
}
}
]
}
```

3. Deploy and Manage Azure Compute Resources (20–25%)

THIS DOMAIN CENTERS around provisioning and managing compute resources such as virtual machines (VMs), scale sets, and containers.

Key Objectives:

- Configure VMs (Linux/Windows)
- Automate deployments using ARM or Bicep templates
- Create and configure virtual machine scale sets (VMSS)

- Configure Azure App Services and container instances
- Manage VM availability (zones, sets), backup, and monitoring

EXAMPLE: DEPLOYING a VM using CLI

az vm create \

—resource-group dev-rg \

—name devvm01 \

—image UbuntuLTS \

—admin-username azureadmin \

—generate-ssh-keys

Example: Configuring auto-scaling for a VMSS

az monitor autoscale create—resource-group dev-rg \

—resource devvmss—resource-type Microsoft.Compute/virtualMachineScaleSets \

—name autoscale-rule—min-count 1—max-count 5—count 2

4. Configure and Manage Virtual Networking (20–25%)

THIS SECTION EMPHASIZES configuring connectivity and securing network traffic using VNets, subnets, VPNs, and NSGs.

Key Objectives:

- Configure virtual networks, subnets, and peering

- Configure public and private IP addressing
- Secure network traffic using NSGs and Azure Firewall
- Configure Azure DNS, Bastion, and VPN gateways
- Monitor and troubleshoot networking issues

EXAMPLE: CREATING A virtual network

```
az network vnet create \
—name prod-vnet \
—resource-group prod-rg \
—subnet-name web-subnet
```

Example: Implementing NSG for subnet

```
az network nsg rule create \
—resource-group prod-rg \
—nsg-name web-nsg \
—name AllowHTTP \
—protocol Tcp—direction Inbound—priority 100 \
—source-address-prefixes '*' \
—destination-port-ranges 80 \
—access Allow
```

5. Monitor and Back Up Azure Resources (10–15%)

THIS DOMAIN IS FOCUSED on monitoring infrastructure health, creating alerts, setting up backups, and managing recovery.

Key Objectives:

- Configure and interpret metrics and logs
- Set up alerts using Azure Monitor
- Configure diagnostic settings and workspace integration
- Implement backup policies using Recovery Services Vault
- Use Azure Advisor and Cost Management

EXAMPLE: ENABLING DIAGNOSTIC logs for a storage account

az monitor diagnostic-settings create \

—name "diagStorageLogs" \

—resource "/subscriptions/<sub-id>/resourceGroups/prod-rg/providers/Microsoft.Storage/storageAccounts/mystorageacct" \

—workspace "<log-analytics-workspace-id>" \

—logs '[{"category": "StorageRead", "enabled": true}]'

Example: Creating a backup policy

az backup policy create \

—resource-group prod-rg \

—vault-name prod-vault \

—name daily-backup-policy \

—policy
'{"backupManagementType":"AzureIaasVM","schedulePolicy":{"scheduleRu

---

Exam Preparation Resources

TO HELP CANDIDATES prepare, Microsoft and other third parties offer a range of resources:

- **Microsoft Learn**: Free, interactive modules aligned with exam objectives
- **Exam Sandbox**: Simulated environment to experience exam interface
- **Official Practice Tests**: Provided by MeasureUp or Pearson
- **Books and Study Guides**: Such as this guide
- **Instructor-led Training**: Microsoft Certified Trainers (MCTs)
- **Community Forums and Study Groups**: Microsoft Tech Community, Reddit, Discord

---

Exam Changes and Updates

MICROSOFT FREQUENTLY updates exam content to reflect changes in Azure services. It is critical to:

- Review theofficial skills outline[1] before preparing.
- Practice in a real or sandbox Azure environment.
- Use updated tools (e.g., Bicep instead of JSON ARM where appropriate).

Summary

THE AZ-104 EXAM IS a robust measure of a candidate's ability to manage and administer Azure environments across identity, compute, storage, networking, and monitoring. Understanding the scope and structure of the exam is foundational for building a strong study plan and aligning your technical skills with real-world administrative responsibilities. As the industry demand for cloud professionals grows, mastering the AZ-104 objectives ensures you're prepared to contribute to any Azure-based project or environment with confidence and capability.

How to Use This Book Effectively

THIS BOOK IS STRUCTURED to serve both as a comprehensive exam preparation guide and as a reference for real-world Azure administration. Whether you're a first-time candidate for the AZ-104 exam or a working IT professional aiming to deepen your Azure knowledge, understanding how to navigate and utilize this book is critical to your success.

Structuring Your Learning Path

THE CONTENT IN THIS book aligns directly with the official skills measured in the AZ-104 exam and mirrors the structure of a

---

1. https://learn.microsoft.com/en-us/certifications/exams/az-104/

real Azure environment. Each chapter focuses on one major domain of Azure administration and corresponds to an AZ-104 exam section.

To maximize the effectiveness of your study:

- **Read Chapters Sequentially**: Begin with Chapter 1 and progress through the book in order. Each chapter builds on the previous one, reinforcing your understanding incrementally.

- **Use the Learning Objectives**: Each section maps to specific skills tested on the exam. Pay close attention to headings and subheadings—they are reflective of Microsoft's exam blueprint.

- **Practice After Reading**: After reading a section, immediately implement what you've learned in an Azure subscription. Whether it's creating a resource group or deploying a VM, hands-on practice is crucial.

- **Review Key Terms**: Highlighted terms and concepts appear frequently in exam questions. These are also defined in the glossary in Chapter 9 for easy revision.

- **Take Notes and Use Mind Maps**: Personal notes and visual aids like mind maps can reinforce memory retention and help summarize complex topics.

Navigating Chapter Structure

EACH CHAPTER IN THIS book is organized using a consistent format to help streamline your study:

- **Overview**: A brief introduction to the focus of the chapter and how it aligns with the AZ-104 objectives.

- **Deep Dive Content**: Detailed explanations, conceptual walkthroughs, diagrams (in referenced materials), and code samples using Azure CLI, PowerShell, Bicep, or JSON.

- **Real-World Scenarios**: Practical applications and case studies that show how the concepts are used in enterprise settings.

- **Practice Exercises**: At the end of most sections, you'll find sample CLI commands, configurations, or short tasks to help solidify your learning.

- **Review Questions**: Available in Chapter 7, you can use these to assess your understanding and identify areas needing more focus.

Recommended Study Workflow

1. **Assess Your Baseline Knowledge**: Start by scanning the AZ-104 skills outline. Mark areas you're unfamiliar with.

2. **Allocate Time per Chapter**: Each chapter may require several hours depending on your experience level. For example:

   - Chapter 2 (Identities and Governance): 6–8 hours

   - Chapter 4 (Compute Resources): 8–10 hours

3. **Read with Purpose**: Focus on concepts, then details. Use annotations or digital notes if reading on a device.

4. **Implement in Azure**: Sign up for an Azure free account if needed, and use it for practice.

5. **Take Practice Quizzes**: After every major section, use the test questions in Chapter 7 to measure your retention.

6. **Reinforce Through Repetition**: Return to tricky topics after a day or two. Repetition builds mastery.

Utilizing Practice Labs and Scripts

THIS BOOK FREQUENTLY includes commands and snippets that you can run directly in your Azure environment. Here's how to set up your own lab:

- **Create a Free Azure Account**: Visithttps://azure.microsoft.com[2] and sign up for the free tier, which includes credits and always-free services.

- **Use Cloud Shell**: This browser-based CLI interface requires no setup and supports both Bash and PowerShell.

Organize Labs by Resource Groups:

az group create—name AZ104-Lab1—location uksouth

- This makes it easier to delete and clean up labs after completing them.

2. https://azure.microsoft.com/

- **Keep Reusable Scripts**: Store your CLI commands and Bicep templates in a GitHub repo or cloud-based note system for future use and study.

Balancing Theory and Practice

UNDERSTANDING AZURE is not just about memorizing commands; it's about understanding *why* a particular feature exists and *how* it fits into the broader architecture. For example:

- When studying NSGs (Network Security Groups), don't just learn how to create one—understand how it impacts traffic flow, its place in the OSI model, and how it differs from Azure Firewall.

- In the context of storage, know the practical implications of replication tiers (LRS vs. GRS) and when to use which.

Use this book to create connections between conceptual understanding and technical implementation.

Study Techniques to Reinforce Learning

THE FOLLOWING TECHNIQUES can dramatically improve your comprehension and retention:

- **Spaced Repetition**: Review topics over increasing intervals (e.g., Day 1, Day 3, Day 7).

- **Flashcards**: Create digital cards for key terms, CLI flags, and command syntax.

- **Teach What You Learn**: Explain a concept (e.g., virtual network peering) to someone else or write a blog post about it.

- **Self-Testing**: Use end-of-section questions or platforms like MeasureUp to simulate exam conditions.

- **Error-Driven Learning**: Make mistakes during practice labs and troubleshoot the issues—this is often more instructive than getting it right the first time.

How to Approach the Exam with This Book

TOWARD THE END OF YOUR preparation, focus specifically on Chapter 7, which includes:

- A customizable 30-day study plan

- A breakdown of question types and how to approach them

- Mind maps and one-pagers for last-minute review

- A "mock exam" section with explanations for each answer

Use this content as your final checkpoint before scheduling your exam date.

Tips for Ongoing Use Post-Certification

THIS BOOK IS NOT ONLY a certification prep tool; it's also designed for long-term use as a reference manual.

- **Bookmark Chapters**: Especially for tasks like backup configuration, App Service scaling, or ARM deployments.

- **Use as an Onboarding Tool**: If you're leading a team, this book can be a structured guide for onboarding junior admins.

- **Stay Current**: Microsoft Azure evolves rapidly. Bookmark the official documentation and use this book's structure as a mental model to organize your ongoing learning.

Common Pitfalls to Avoid

- **Skipping Practice**: Reading alone will not prepare you adequately. Azure is a platform where theory without practice fails.

- **Memorizing Instead of Understanding**: Understand the principles behind services and settings.

- **Overloading Study Sessions**: Aim for deep focus over long hours. A single well-understood topic is more valuable than skimming multiple ones.

IGNORING COSTS: Running VMs or other non-free services can incur charges. Always delete unused resources:

az group delete—name AZ104-Lab1—yes—no-wait

-

Summary

THIS BOOK IS YOUR ROADMAP to becoming a skilled Azure Administrator. It's designed to meet you at your current skill level and elevate you through a structured, practical, and comprehensive learning journey. Use it as a study companion, a lab guide, a post-certification reference, and a long-term resource throughout your Azure career. By reading, practicing, and reflecting deeply, you will not only pass the AZ-104 exam—you will thrive in real-world Azure environments.

Chapter 2: Managing Azure Identities and Governance

Managing Azure Active Directory (Azure AD)

AZURE ACTIVE DIRECTORY (Azure AD) is Microsoft's cloud-based identity and access management service. It plays a central role in securing user identities and managing authentication and authorization across all Azure resources and Microsoft 365 services. For an Azure Administrator, understanding how to configure and manage Azure AD is foundational to securing an organization's cloud infrastructure and enabling productivity without compromising control.

What Is Azure Active Directory?

AZURE AD IS NOT JUST an extension of on-premises Active Directory (AD); it is a cloud-native directory service that supports modern identity features including single sign-on (SSO), multifactor authentication (MFA), device management, and conditional access. Azure AD enables employees, customers, and partners to securely access internal and external resources using one identity.

It is used to:

- Authenticate and authorize access to Azure resources
- Integrate with SaaS applications like Microsoft 365, Salesforce, and Dropbox
- Manage users and groups, including hybrid identity from on-premises AD

- Apply security policies such as conditional access and MFA
- Integrate with identity providers like Google, Facebook, or enterprise SAML/WS-Fed providers

Azure AD Tenants and Directories

WHEN YOU CREATE AN Azure account, a default Azure AD tenant (or directory) is automatically created. This tenant is associated with the organization and governs access to all Azure subscriptions tied to it.

Each Azure AD tenant:

- Is globally unique and assigned a domain like yourcompany.onmicrosoft.com
- Can have custom domains added (e.g., yourcompany.com)
- Can be synced with on-premises Active Directory using Azure AD Connect
- Contains users, groups, enterprise applications, and policies

You can manage tenants in the Azure Portal under **Azure Active Directory** or via CLI:

```
az account tenant list
```

Users, Groups, and Devices

Managing Users

USERS CAN BE CREATED manually, synchronized from on-premises AD, or federated through external identity providers.

To create a user manually using Azure CLI:

az ad user create \

—display-name "Alice Smith" \

—user-principal-name alice@yourdomain.com \

—password "P@ssword123" \

—force-change-password-next-login true

You can also use the Azure Portal for graphical creation and management, or PowerShell for batch operations.

Managing Groups

GROUPS ARE A KEY PART of access control in Azure. They allow you to assign permissions or roles to multiple users efficiently. Azure AD supports:

- **Security Groups** – Used for managing access to Azure resources
- **Microsoft 365 Groups** – Include shared mailbox, calendar, SharePoint site, and Planner

To create a security group using CLI:

```
az ad group create \
—display-name "DevOps Team" \
—mail-nickname "devops"
```

To add a user to a group:

```
az ad group member add \
—group "DevOps Team" \
—member-id <user-object-id>
```

Managing Devices

AZURE AD ALSO MANAGES devices such as Windows, macOS, iOS, and Android machines. Devices can be:

- Azure AD Registered (for personal BYOD)
- Azure AD Joined (for corporate-owned)
- Hybrid Azure AD Joined (on-prem AD joined and registered in Azure AD)

Device registration helps enforce compliance policies, conditional access, and seamless SSO.

Hybrid Identity with Azure AD Connect

AZURE AD CONNECT IS the bridge between on-premises Active Directory and Azure AD. It synchronizes user identities and optionally enables federated authentication with services like ADFS.

Modes of authentication supported by Azure AD Connect:

- **Password Hash Synchronization (PHS)**
- **Pass-through Authentication (PTA)**
- **Federation (e.g., ADFS)**

For most organizations, PHS is recommended for simplicity and reduced overhead.

Basic installation command on a Windows Server:

.\AzureADConnect.msi

Configuration options include:

- Selecting OUs for sync
- Filtering groups
- Enabling seamless SSO

Azure AD Connect can also write back attributes like passwords or groups to on-premises AD (if writeback is enabled).

External Identities and B2B Collaboration

AZURE AD SUPPORTS EXTERNAL collaboration through Azure AD B2B (Business-to-Business). This allows organizations to invite partners or contractors to access resources without creating full accounts.

To invite a guest user:

az ad user invite \

—user-principal-name guest@example.com \

—invite-redirect-url https://myapp.com/welcome

Guest users can be restricted via Conditional Access and limited to specific roles or applications.

Identity Protection and Conditional Access

AZURE AD INCLUDES ADVANCED security tools to detect risky logins and enforce access control policies.

Conditional Access

POLICIES ARE USED TO enforce rules such as requiring MFA if accessing from an unknown location or device.

Example policy: Require MFA for admins logging in outside the UK.

Steps:

1. Go to **Azure AD** → **Security** → **Conditional Access**
2. Create a new policy:
   - **Users**: Directory roles → Global Administrator
   - **Cloud apps**: All
   - **Conditions**: Location → exclude UK
   - **Access controls**: Require multifactor authentication

Identity Protection

PROVIDES RISK-BASED identity management:

- Detects risky sign-ins (e.g., impossible travel, leaked credentials)

- Detects risky users

- Automates remediation (e.g., password reset, blocking sign-in)

Azure AD P2 is required for full Identity Protection features.

Authentication Methods

AZURE AD SUPPORTS VARIOUS authentication methods:

- **Password-based**

- **Multi-Factor Authentication (MFA)**

- **Windows Hello for Business**

- **FIDO2 security keys**

- **Certificate-based authentication**

- **Temporary Access Pass (TAP)**

Admins can manage these under **Azure AD → Security → Authentication Methods**.

Enable TAP for break-glass access:

```
Set-AzureADPolicy -Definition
@("{'TemporaryAccessPassPolicies':[{'isUsableOnce':true,'lifetimeInMinut
-DisplayName "TAPPolicy" -IsOrganizationDefault $true
```

Enterprise Applications and SSO

AZURE AD ENABLES SINGLE sign-on to thousands of pre-integrated SaaS apps. Administrators can:

- Configure SAML, OAuth, or OpenID Connect apps
- Assign users or groups
- Control app access with conditional access policies
- Monitor usage and sign-ins

Example: Configuring Salesforce SSO using SAML involves:

- Adding Salesforce from the Azure AD gallery
- Downloading the Federation Metadata XML
- Uploading it to Salesforce and matching claims
- Testing and enabling the application

Best Practices for Managing Azure AD

- **Use groups, not individuals**, for role assignments
- **Implement MFA** for all users, especially admins
- **Enable Conditional Access policies** early
- **Monitor sign-ins** and audit logs regularly
- **Use Azure AD Connect health** to monitor sync issues

- **Separate break-glass accounts** with MFA excluded for emergencies
- **Restrict user consent** for apps to prevent shadow IT risks

Summary

MANAGING AZURE ACTIVE Directory is foundational to administering a secure and scalable Azure environment. From handling user lifecycles and group memberships to configuring hybrid identities and conditional access, Azure AD empowers organizations to centralize identity management across cloud and on-premises environments. For an Azure Administrator, mastering Azure AD is not optional—it is essential to enforcing governance, maintaining compliance, and protecting the modern enterprise from identity-based threats.

Role-Based Access Control (RBAC)

ROLE-BASED ACCESS CONTROL (RBAC) is a fundamental security mechanism in Microsoft Azure that allows administrators to manage user permissions for Azure resources in a granular and scalable way. Instead of assigning permissions directly to users, RBAC enables assigning roles to users, groups, service principals, or managed identities at different scopes. This ensures that individuals or systems can only access the resources they are authorized to interact with, enforcing the principle of least privilege across the cloud environment.

Understanding RBAC

RBAC WORKS BY COMBINING three core elements:

- **Security Principal**: The identity requesting access (user, group, service principal, or managed identity).

- **Role Definition**: A collection of permissions like read, write, delete, or list. Azure provides built-in roles, and you can also create custom roles.

- **Scope**: The set of resources the role applies to, such as a subscription, resource group, or specific resource.

RBAC evaluates whether a security principal has access by checking the assigned roles at all levels of the scope hierarchy.

Hierarchy Level	Description
Management Group	Container for multiple subscriptions
Subscription	Billing boundary and container for resources
Resource Group	Logical container for related resources
Resource	The actual service (e.g., VM, Storage)

If a role is assigned at a broader scope, it is inherited by all child scopes unless explicitly overridden.

Built-In Roles

AZURE INCLUDES OVER 100 built-in roles designed for common job functions. Some widely used roles include:

Role Name	Description
Owner	Full access to manage all resources including RBAC
Contributor	Full access to manage resources, but not RBAC permissions
Reader	View resources but no actions
User Access Administrator	Manage user access to Azure resources
Virtual Machine Contributor	Manage VMs but not the network or storage
Storage Blob Data Reader	Read access to blobs and containers in storage accounts

Example: Assigning the **Contributor** role to a user at the resource group level gives them permission to manage all resources in that group, but not to assign roles.

Assigning a Role with the Azure Portal

1. Navigate to the resource (e.g., a Resource Group).
2. Click **Access control (IAM).**
3. Select + **Add** → **Add role assignment.**
4. Choose a role (e.g., Reader), assign access to a user, and confirm.

THIS ROLE IS NOW EFFECTIVE at the scope you chose and inherited by child resources.

Assigning a Role Using Azure CLI

TO ASSIGN THE READER role at a resource group level:

```
az role assignment create \
```

—assignee "user@domain.com" \

—role "Reader" \

—resource-group "dev-rg"

To list current assignments:

az role assignment list—assignee "user@domain.com"

To remove a role assignment:

az role assignment delete \

—assignee "user@domain.com" \

—role "Reader" \

—resource-group "dev-rg"

Custom Roles

BUILT-IN ROLES MAY not always align perfectly with your organization's needs. Azure allows creation of **custom roles** to define precise permissions.

A custom role is a JSON object containing:

- **Name**
- **Description**
- **Actions** (e.g., Microsoft.Compute/virtualMachines/start/action)
- **NotActions** (e.g., explicitly deny permissions)
- **AssignableScopes** (e.g., /subscriptions/abc123)

Example JSON:

```
{
"Name": "Custom VM Starter",
"IsCustom": true,
"Description": "Can start and stop virtual machines.",
"Actions": [
"Microsoft.Compute/virtualMachines/start/action",
"Microsoft.Compute/virtualMachines/deallocate/action"
],
"NotActions": [],
"AssignableScopes": ["/subscriptions/abc123"]
}
```

Create the role using Azure CLI:

```
az role definition create—role-definition ./customrole.json
```

Role Assignment Best Practices

- **Use Groups over Users**: Assign roles to security groups rather than individual users to simplify access control.
- **Adopt the Principle of Least Privilege**: Grant only the permissions required for the job.
- **Audit Role Assignments Regularly**: Remove redundant or outdated role assignments.

- **Tag Role Assignments**: Use tags to identify purpose or project context.
- **Use Conditional Access for Additional Contextual Control**: Combine RBAC with conditional access for location/device-based control.

Viewing Effective Permissions

YOU CAN VIEW THE EFFECTIVE permissions of a user on a particular resource using:

- **Azure Portal**: Access control → Check access → Select user → View permissions.
- **Azure CLI**:

az role assignment list—assignee "user@domain.com"

This helps verify what a user can do across different scopes and is useful for troubleshooting access issues.

Scenarios and Examples

Scenario 1: DevOps Engineer for a Specific App

YOU WANT TO ALLOW A DevOps engineer to manage VMs but not touch the network or storage.

Solution: Assign Virtual Machine Contributor at the resource group level:

az role assignment create \

—assignee "devops@yourdomain.com" \

—role "Virtual Machine Contributor" \

—resource-group "app-rg"

Scenario 2: Read-Only Access for Auditors

A COMPLIANCE TEAM NEEDS to view Azure configurations but must not change anything.

Solution: Assign the Reader role at the subscription level:

az role assignment create \

—assignee "auditor@yourdomain.com" \

—role "Reader" \

—scope "/subscriptions/abc123"

Scenario 3: Custom Role for Backup Operators

A TEAM IS RESPONSIBLE only for managing backups. Built-in roles provide too many permissions.

Solution: Create a custom role with permissions like:

"Actions": [

"Microsoft.RecoveryServices/vaults/backupFabrics/backupProtectionIntent/write",

"Microsoft.RecoveryServices/vaults/backupPolicies/read",

"Microsoft.RecoveryServices/vaults/backupJobs/read"

]

Apply this custom role at the resource group level containing Recovery Services Vaults.

RBAC vs Azure Policy

RBAC IS CONCERNED WITH **who** can do **what** at a specific scope, whereas **Azure Policy** governs **what** can be done, irrespective of who attempts the action.

Feature	**RBAC**	**Azure Policy**
Focus	Permissions	Resource compliance and control
Use Case	Grant access to resources	Enforce rules and effects (e.g., allowed SKUs)
Enforcement	Denies actions not explicitly allowed	Evaluates and blocks or audits deployments

They are often used together—RBAC controls access, and Policy controls behavior.

Troubleshooting Role-Based Access Issues

IF A USER CANNOT ACCESS a resource:

1. Check if the user has any roles assigned at the required scope.
2. Check if permissions are being blocked by a **deny assignment.**
3. Validate if inheritance is broken by a more restrictive role at a child scope.
4. Use az role assignment list or the portal to inspect current assignments.
5. Ensure correct object ID is used when assigning to service principals.

Auditing and Monitoring Access

USE AZURE ACTIVITY Logs and Azure Monitor to track:

- Role changes
- Unauthorized access attempts
- Changes to resource permissions

Enable alerts for unexpected modifications to IAM configurations using Azure Monitor.

Set up a diagnostic setting:

```
az monitor diagnostic-settings create \

—name "AuditIAMChanges" \

—resource "/subscriptions/abc123" \

—workspace <LogAnalyticsWorkspaceID> \

—logs '[{"category": "Administrative", "enabled": true}]'
```

Summary

ROLE-BASED ACCESS CONTROL is a critical framework for managing secure and scalable access in Azure. By understanding how RBAC works, what scopes and roles exist, and how to create custom definitions, Azure Administrators can enforce strict access controls, reduce risk, and streamline resource management. Mastering RBAC not only helps in passing the AZ-104 exam but is vital for any real-world Azure deployment that values governance and compliance.

Subscriptions and Management Groups

AZURE'S HIERARCHICAL structure is designed to provide both flexibility and control for organizing resources across large environments. At the heart of this structure are **subscriptions** and **management groups**, two foundational concepts for governance, resource organization, billing, and access control. Understanding how to use them effectively allows Azure administrators to scale environments, enforce policy, and structure cloud usage to meet the needs of complex organizations.

Understanding Subscriptions

A **subscription** is a logical container used to provision resources in Microsoft Azure. Each subscription holds a set of resources that are billed together. Subscriptions serve as:

- A **billing unit**: All usage within a subscription is aggregated into a single invoice.

- A **security boundary**: Role assignments, policies, and permissions are scoped at the subscription level.

- A **management boundary**: Resources in one subscription are isolated from those in another unless explicitly connected.

An organization may use a single subscription or many, depending on requirements such as:

- Departmental separation (e.g., IT, Marketing, Finance)

- Environment segmentation (e.g., Development, QA, Production)

- Legal or regulatory isolation
- Billing ownership or chargeback mechanisms

Types of Azure Subscriptions

AZURE OFFERS SEVERAL types of subscriptions, including:

Subscription Type	Description
Pay-As-You-Go	Standard subscription with consumption-based billing
Azure Free Trial	Offers credits to try Azure services
Enterprise Agreement (EA)	For large organizations with volume licensing
Microsoft Customer Agreement (MCA)	New billing model with consolidated management
CSP (Cloud Solution Provider)	Managed by a third-party reseller
Visual Studio (MSDN)	Developer subscription with monthly credit allowance

You can view your current subscriptions using:

az account list—output table

To set the default subscription:

az account set—subscription "Subscription Name or ID"

Creating and Managing Subscriptions

AZURE SUBSCRIPTIONS are usually created through the Azure Portal, CSP partner portal, or EA portal. However, administrators can manage them using Azure CLI and PowerShell for scripting tasks like associating resources, switching subscriptions, and applying policies.

Each subscription is associated with an **Azure Active Directory tenant** and can be moved between management groups but cannot be arbitrarily moved between tenants.

To manage a subscription programmatically:

az account show

To switch context:

az account set—subscription "MyProdSubscription"

To check which resources are deployed under a subscription:

az resource list—subscription "MyProdSubscription"

Resource Organization: The Role of Resource Groups

EACH AZURE SUBSCRIPTION contains one or more **resource groups**, which are logical containers for resources like VMs, databases, and networks. Resource groups allow for:

- Unified lifecycle management (e.g., delete all resources in a group)
- Scoped permissions using RBAC
- Tagging and billing segmentation

Although resource groups are within subscriptions, they are pivotal in organizing infrastructure.

az group create—name app-rg—location uksouth

Resources can be moved between resource groups within the same subscription, but cross-subscription movement has limitations and considerations, especially for dependent services.

What Are Management Groups?

MANAGEMENT GROUPS are containers that help you efficiently manage access, policy, and compliance across multiple Azure subscriptions. They allow you to organize subscriptions into a hierarchy and apply governance consistently.

Key Characteristics:

- Every management group is part of a **single hierarchy** rooted at the **Tenant Root Group**.
- Each group can contain multiple subscriptions or child management groups.
- RBAC and Azure Policy assignments applied at a management group are inherited by child groups and subscriptions.
- Each Azure AD tenant can have up to 10,000 management groups.

Hierarchy Example:

```
Tenant Root Group
│
├── Corp (Management Group)
│ ├── Production (Subscription)
```

│ └── Development (Subscription)

└── Finance (Management Group)

└── Billing (Subscription)

To list management groups:

az account management-group list

To create a management group:

az account management-group create—name "Engineering"—display-name "Engineering Division"

To move a subscription into a management group:

az account management-group subscription add—name "Engineering"—subscription "MyProdSubscription"

Benefits of Management Groups

- **Centralized Policy Enforcement**: Deploy policies at the group level that propagate downward (e.g., only allow VMs in West Europe).

- **Delegated Administration**: Grant RBAC roles at different levels for different teams.

- **Compliance Monitoring**: Apply security and audit requirements at scale.

- **Cost Governance**: Align subscriptions with departments, business units, or projects.

Combining RBAC and Management Groups

RBAC ASSIGNMENTS CAN be made at the management group level to enforce consistent access control across multiple subscriptions.

Example: Assigning a user as a Reader at the management group level:

az role assignment create \

—assignee user@domain.com \

—role "Reader" \

—scope "/providers/Microsoft.Management/managementGroups/Engineering"

This user now has read-only access across all subscriptions within the “Engineering” management group.

Naming Conventions and Tagging Strategies

ESTABLISHING CONSISTENT naming and tagging policies across subscriptions and resource groups simplifies governance and reporting.

Naming Examples:

- Subscriptions: az-prod-networking, az-dev-data
- Resource Groups: rg-prod-app, rg-test-api

Tag Examples:

az tag create—name Environment—value Production

az resource tag—ids <resource-id>—tags Environment=Production CostCenter=IT123

These tags are useful for chargeback models, compliance filtering, and resource discovery.

Azure Policy with Subscriptions and Management Groups

AZURE POLICY CAN BE applied at the management group or subscription level to enforce standards such as:

- Only specific VM sizes allowed
- Require tags on all resources
- Disallow creation of public IPs

Example: Assigning a policy at the management group level:

az policy assignment create \

—name "enforceTags" \

—scope "/providers/Microsoft.Management/managementGroups/Corp" \

—policy "/providers/Microsoft.Authorization/policyDefinitions/enforce-tag"

This policy applies to all child subscriptions, enforcing a consistent security or operational standard.

Subscription Limits and Quotas

EACH SUBSCRIPTION HAS limits, including:

Resource	Limit
Number of VMs per region	Varies by SKU
Resource groups per subscription	980
Management groups per tenant	10,000
Role assignments per subscription	~2,000

These limits can often be increased by submitting a support request in the Azure Portal.

Best Practices for Managing Subscriptions and Management Groups

- **Use Management Groups from Day One**: Avoid retrofitting governance later.
- **Map to Organizational Units**: Align subscriptions with finance, HR, dev teams, etc.
- **Isolate Environments**: Use separate subscriptions for development, staging, and production.
- **Standardize Naming and Tags**: Create a governance document and enforce with policy.
- **Audit Access Regularly**: Use activity logs and RBAC reviews for access hygiene.
- **Leverage Blueprints**: For consistent deployment of resources and policies (note: Azure Blueprints is being deprecated; use ARM templates and policies).

Summary

SUBSCRIPTIONS AND MANAGEMENT groups are critical elements in organizing, securing, and governing Azure environments. Subscriptions offer billing and resource boundaries, while management groups introduce scalable governance structures that can apply security, policy, and access control across many subscriptions at once. For an Azure Administrator, mastering how to structure and manage these layers effectively is essential for enterprise-grade cloud operations and compliance.

Implementing and Managing Policies

AZURE POLICY IS A POWERFUL service that allows organizations to create, assign, and manage policies that enforce rules and effects over Azure resources. These policies help ensure that resources are compliant with corporate standards and regulatory requirements. As organizations scale, maintaining governance becomes more complex—Azure Policy offers an automated, scalable mechanism for defining and controlling resource behavior across subscriptions, resource groups, and management groups.

What Is Azure Policy?

AZURE POLICY IS A GOVERNANCE tool that helps you:

- **Enforce organizational standards** (e.g., enforce specific regions for deployment)
- **Audit resource configurations** (e.g., track untagged resources)
- **Prevent policy violations** before resources are created

- **Remediate non-compliant resources**

Policies are evaluated at resource creation and update time, ensuring real-time enforcement of constraints.

Key Azure Policy Concepts

Concept	Description
Policy Definition	A rule describing the conditions under which a resource is compliant.
Policy Assignment	Applying a policy to a scope (management group, subscription, etc.).
Policy Parameters	Values that can be used to customize a policy (e.g., allowed regions).
Initiatives	A collection of policy definitions grouped into a single assignment.
Effects	The result of policy evaluation (e.g., deny, audit, append, deployIfNotExists).

Policy Structure

AN AZURE POLICY DEFINITION is a JSON object that contains:

- **Mode**: Specifies the type of resource to which the policy applies (e.g., all, indexed, Microsoft.Kubernetes.Data).

- **Parameters**: Input values used when assigning the policy.

- **Rule**: Defines the condition under which the policy applies.

- **Effect**: Describes what action Azure takes when the rule matches.

Example policy to enforce a specific region:

```
{
"properties": {
"displayName": "Allow only UK South region",
"mode": "All",
"parameters": {
"allowedLocations": {
"type": "Array",
"metadata": {
"displayName": "Allowed locations"
}
}
},
"policyRule": {
"if": {
"not": {
"field": "location",
"in": "[parameters('allowedLocations')]"
```

}

},

"then": {

"effect": "deny"

}

}

}

}

You can assign this policy using:

az policy definition create \

—name "allow-uksouth" \

—rules allow-only-uksouth.json \

—params '{"allowedLocations": {"value": ["uksouth"]}}' \

—mode All

Policy Assignment

AFTER DEFINING A POLICY, it must be **assigned** to take effect. Assignments can be made at:

- Management Group level (affects all child subscriptions)
- Subscription level

- Resource Group level

az policy assignment create \

—name "restrict-location" \

—scope "/subscriptions/xxxx-xxxx-xxxx-xxxx" \

—policy "allow-uksouth" \

—params '{"allowedLocations": {"value": ["uksouth"]}}'

You can view assigned policies with:

az policy assignment list—output table

Initiative Definitions

INITIATIVES GROUP RELATED policies to simplify management and compliance reporting.

Example: A security baseline initiative may include:

- Require tag Environment
- Enforce resource location
- Deny public IPs

Create an initiative with:

az policy set-definition create \

—name "security-baseline" \

—definitions policyset.json \

—display-name "Security Compliance Baseline"

Then assign it:

az policy assignment create \

—name "security-baseline-enforce" \

—scope "/subscriptions/xxxx" \

—policy-set-definition "security-baseline"

Effects Explained

AZURE POLICIES USE effects to define what happens when a rule matches. Common effects include:

Effect	Description
Deny	Blocks the operation if non-compliant.
Audit	Logs the non-compliance without blocking.
Append	Adds fields to the resource during creation.
DeployIfNotExists	Deploys a related resource if it's missing.
Disabled	Turns off the policy.

Audit is useful during testing or gradual enforcement, while **Deny** is used when strict control is required.

Policy Evaluation and Compliance

AZURE POLICY EVALUATES resources:

- During creation or update
- Periodically (background scan)
- On-demand via remediation tasks

You can trigger a scan manually:

az policy state trigger-scan—resource "/subscriptions/xxxx"

View compliance results:

az policy state summarize—management-group "Corp"

Or in the Azure Portal under **Policy → Compliance**.

Remediation Tasks

POLICIES WITH THE **DeployIfNotExists** or **Modify** effect can automatically fix non-compliant resources.

Example: Ensure all storage accounts have Secure Transfer enabled.

- Assign a policy with DeployIfNotExists
- Create a **remediation task** to apply the configuration retroactively

az policy remediation create \

—name "fix-insecure-storage" \

—policy-assignment "secure-storage-policy" \

—scope "/subscriptions/xxxx"

Remediation tasks are useful for:

- Automating compliance enforcement
- Updating existing infrastructure
- Avoiding manual intervention

Common Use Cases

Enforce Allowed VM Sizes

RESTRICT TEAMS TO ONLY deploy specific VM sizes (e.g., B-series).

Require Tags

ENSURE ALL RESOURCES have Department, Owner, and Environment tags.

Prevent Public IPs

DENY CREATION OF PUBLIC IP addresses except for whitelisted use cases.

Geo-Compliance

RESTRICT RESOURCE CREATION to approved regions due to legal requirements.

Enforce Secure Configurations

REQUIRE DIAGNOSTICS settings on VMs, encryption on storage, HTTPS-only traffic on App Services.

Policy vs RBAC

IT'S IMPORTANT TO DISTINGUISH Azure Policy from Role-Based Access Control:

Feature	Azure Policy	RBAC
What it controls	Resource properties and configurations	Who has access and what they can do
Effect type	Prevents or audits actions	Grants permissions
Evaluated	Continuously and at creation time	At request time

Used together, these tools enable robust governance and access control.

Best Practices for Policy Management

- **Start with Audit**: Monitor violations before applying Deny.
- **Use Initiatives**: Group related policies for easier management.
- **Use Parameters**: Increase reusability by parameterizing region, tags, etc.
- **Apply at Higher Scope**: Assign policies at management group level to enforce consistency.
- **Document Policies**: Maintain a policy registry with purpose, owners, and update history.
- **Version Policies**: For custom definitions, use version control systems like Git.

Monitoring and Alerts

AZURE MONITOR INTEGRATES with Policy to trigger alerts on policy violations. You can:

- Send alerts to email or ITSM
- Trigger Logic Apps or runbooks
- Visualize compliance trends over time

Example: Alert on any resource missing a required tag.

Create a log query:

PolicyResources

| where IsCompliant == false and PolicyDefinitionName == "Require Tags"

1.

2. Pin results to a dashboard or configure an alert rule.

Summary

AZURE POLICY IS A CENTRAL tool in the Azure governance model. It allows administrators to define and enforce organizational standards across an entire Azure environment. With capabilities such as denying non-compliant resources, auditing changes, auto-remediation, and aggregating compliance data, Azure Policy transforms governance from a manual to an automated process. By mastering its use, Azure Administrators can ensure environments remain compliant, secure, and aligned with business and regulatory requirements at scale.

Monitoring and Reporting Access

MONITORING AND REPORTING access to Azure resources is a critical responsibility for ensuring security, maintaining compliance, and auditing usage across the cloud environment. Azure offers a comprehensive suite of tools and services to track who has access to what, how that access is being used, and whether it aligns with your organizational governance policies.

As environments grow in complexity—with multiple subscriptions, hundreds of users, and automated service principals—it becomes essential for administrators to adopt continuous access monitoring strategies to detect anomalies, prevent privilege escalation, and maintain control over cloud resources.

Why Monitor Access?

ACCESS MONITORING ENSURES that:

- Permissions are not overly permissive (violating least privilege).
- Unauthorized users are not accessing sensitive resources.
- Role assignments are intentional, traceable, and auditable.
- Changes in access control (e.g., RBAC) are logged for compliance.
- External or guest user activity is tracked.
- Credential misuse, especially in service principals, can be detected.

By proactively monitoring access and creating reports, organizations can prevent data breaches, meet regulatory requirements, and respond quickly to security incidents.

Key Tools for Access Monitoring in Azure

AZURE PROVIDES A RANGE of native tools and services for monitoring and reporting access:

Tool/Service	Purpose
Azure Activity Logs	Logs all write operations (PUT, POST, DELETE) in the control plane.
Azure AD Sign-in Logs	Tracks user and service principal sign-ins across Azure and Microsoft 365.
Azure AD Audit Logs	Captures identity-related events (user creation, group changes, role assignments).
Azure Monitor & Log Analytics	Centralizes and queries access logs across Azure services.
Microsoft Defender for Cloud	Identifies access risks and misconfigurations.
Access Reviews	Periodic evaluations of user access rights.
Privileged Identity Management (PIM)	Manages, monitors, and justifies privileged access.

Monitoring Role Assignments with Activity Logs

AZURE ACTIVITY LOGS provide detailed tracking of management operations across subscriptions, including all changes to RBAC and policy assignments.

Key log categories related to access:

- Microsoft.Authorization/roleAssignments/write
- Microsoft.Authorization/roleAssignments/delete
- Microsoft.Authorization/roleDefinitions/write

To view role assignment changes using Azure CLI:

az monitor activity-log list \

—resource-group "example-rg" \

—max-events 50 \

—query "[?operationName.value=='Microsoft.Authorization/roleAssignments/write']"

To enable centralized collection:

1. Create a Log Analytics workspace.
2. Configure Diagnostic Settings for Azure Activity Logs.
3. Forward logs to the workspace.

az monitor diagnostic-settings create \

—name "sendActivityToLogAnalytics" \

—resource "/subscriptions/xxxxx" \

—workspace "/subscriptions/xxxxx/resourceGroups/logs-rg/providers/Microsoft.OperationalInsights/workspaces/logs-ws" \

—logs '[{"category": "Administrative", "enabled": true}]'

Azure Active Directory Sign-In Logs

SIGN-IN LOGS HELP DETECT:

- Unusual login patterns (e.g., impossible travel)
- Sign-in attempts from unknown locations
- Failed sign-ins (e.g., MFA failures)
- Legacy authentication use

To query sign-ins using Log Analytics:

```
SigninLogs

| where ResultType != 0

| project UserPrincipalName, IPAddress, AppDisplayName, ResultDescription, TimeGenerated
```

Exporting Sign-In Logs:

- Available via Azure AD → Sign-In Logs
- Exportable to Log Analytics, Storage Account, or Event Hub
- Retention defaults: 7 days (free), 30–365 days (paid plans)

Enable continuous export for audit:

```
az monitor diagnostic-settings create \

—name "aadSignInExport" \

—resource "/providers/Microsoft.aadiam/diagnosticSettings/AzureAD" \

—workspace "<log-analytics-resource-id>" \

—logs '[{"category": "SignInLogs", "enabled": true}]'
```

Azure AD Audit Logs

AUDIT LOGS RECORD CHANGES to identity and access objects, such as:

- User creation/deletion
- Group membership changes
- Role assignments and removals
- Password resets
- Conditional Access changes

Audit Log Use Cases:

- Track who added a user to the Global Administrator role.
- Identify when an external user was invited to the tenant.
- Detect frequent password reset attempts.

Query Example:

```
AuditLogs

| where ActivityDisplayName contains "Add member to group"

| project ActivityDateTime, InitiatedBy.user.displayName, TargetResources[0].displayName
```

Audit logs are critical for root-cause analysis after a security incident.

Access Reviews and Compliance Reporting

AZURE AD ACCESS REVIEWS (requires Azure AD Premium P2) provide a structured method to periodically review and validate user access.

Use cases:

- Ensure only appropriate users retain access to sensitive resources.
- Automate access revocation for inactive or external users.
- Support compliance with standards like ISO 27001, HIPAA, and SOX.

To configure an access review:

1. Go to **Azure AD** → **Identity Governance** → **Access Reviews.**
2. Select a group, application, or role to review.
3. Choose reviewers (e.g., managers, group owners).
4. Set recurrence (e.g., monthly, quarterly).
5. Enable automatic removal of unapproved access.

Access review results are auditable and exportable for compliance evidence.

Privileged Identity Management (PIM)

PIM ENHANCES ACCESS security by:

- Enforcing **just-in-time (JIT)** role activation.
- Requiring approval workflows for elevation.
- Enforcing MFA for role activation.
- Logging activation history and changes.

Configure PIM for RBAC roles:

1. Enable PIM for your directory.
2. Assign eligible users for roles.
3. Set activation conditions (approval, MFA, etc.).

Activation Example:

- User requests access to Contributor role.
- Admin receives approval prompt.
- Upon approval, access is granted for a limited time.
- PIM logs this activity for future auditing.

Defender for Cloud: Identity and Access Insights

MICROSOFT DEFENDER for Cloud (formerly Azure Security Center) analyzes identity configurations and surfaces potential risks such as:

- External accounts with high privileges.
- Roles assigned to unmanaged service principals.
- Legacy authentication usage.
- Missing MFA for privileged accounts.

Access recommendations and alerts are categorized by severity and can trigger automated responses via Azure Logic Apps.

Enable Defender for Identity in:

Microsoft Defender for Cloud → Environment Settings → Enable Identity Recommendations

---

Reporting and Visualization

USE **Azure Monitor Workbooks** to create dashboards combining sign-in logs, audit logs, and role assignments.

Example Workbook Panels:

- Top 10 users by sign-ins
- Failed sign-ins by IP/location
- RBAC changes in the last 30 days
- Role assignment change heatmap

Use Log Analytics queries as data sources and export results as CSV or PDFs for compliance reporting.

Alerts and Automation

AZURE MONITOR ENABLES custom alerts on specific access patterns or changes.

Example: Alert on new role assignment to Owner

1. Create an activity log alert:
    - Operation Name: Microsoft.Authorization/roleAssignments/write
    - RoleDefinitionId: Matches "Owner"
2. Trigger action group:

- Email security team
- Launch runbook to verify user

Use Terraform or Bicep to codify alert rules and integrate them with CI/CD pipelines for governance-as-code.

Best Practices for Access Monitoring

- **Centralize Logs**: Forward all logs to a central Log Analytics workspace.
- **Use PIM for Elevated Roles**: Avoid permanent assignments for sensitive roles.
- **Review Access Periodically**: Conduct quarterly access reviews, especially for guest users.
- **Automate Alerts**: Set alerts for suspicious access patterns or privilege escalations.
- **Limit Role Scope**: Prefer assigning roles at the least privileged scope.
- **Integrate SIEM**: Connect Azure logs to tools like Microsoft Sentinel or Splunk for unified threat detection.

Summary

MONITORING AND REPORTING access is essential for enforcing the principle of least privilege, responding to threats, and achieving regulatory compliance. Azure provides a robust ecosystem of tools—Activity Logs, Sign-In Logs, PIM, Access Reviews, and more—that allow administrators to observe, audit, and control access behavior across the cloud landscape. By integrating these services into a unified strategy, Azure Administrators can maintain visibility, reduce risk, and ensure secure operations at scale.

Chapter 3: Implementing and Managing Storage

Creating and Configuring Storage Accounts

IN MICROSOFT AZURE, storage accounts are foundational components that provide access to scalable, durable, and highly available storage for a variety of data types including blobs, files, queues, and tables. They are a key building block for most cloud solutions—from hosting static websites and backups to managing virtual machine disks and logging telemetry.

As an Azure Administrator, mastering storage accounts means understanding not only how to create them, but also how to configure them with performance, security, replication, and cost considerations in mind.

Types of Azure Storage Accounts

AZURE OFFERS SEVERAL types of storage accounts, each optimized for specific workloads and use cases:

Storage Account Type	Description
General-purpose v2 (GPv2)	The recommended and most versatile type; supports all data services.
General-purpose v1 (GPv1)	Legacy version; fewer features and less cost-effective than GPv2.
BlobStorage	Specialized for block blob and append blob storage only.
FileStorage	Optimized for Azure File shares with premium performance tiers.
BlockBlobStorage	Premium performance tier for block blobs; supports hot/cool access.

For most workloads, **GPv2** is the default and recommended option as it supports the full suite of Azure Storage services, including blob, file, queue, and table storage.

Storage Performance Tiers

PERFORMANCE TIERS AFFECT speed, durability, and cost. Azure offers two primary performance tiers:

- **Standard (HDD-based)**: Cost-effective, suitable for most workloads.
- **Premium (SSD-based)**: Designed for I/O-intensive workloads like databases and big data analytics.

Blob and file storage support **access tiers** that affect how data is stored and priced:

Access Tier	Use Case	Retrieval Latency	Storage Cost	Access Cost
Hot	Frequently accessed data	Low	Higher	Low
Cool	Infrequently accessed data	Slightly higher	Lower	Higher
Archive	Rarely accessed, archival storage	High (hours)	Lowest	Highest

Use access tiers to optimize for cost, especially in scenarios with large volumes of unstructured data.

Creating a Storage Account

Azure Portal

1. Navigate to **Storage accounts → Create.**
2. Select a **resource group**, **region**, and **storage account name.**
3. Choose **performance**, **replication**, and **access tier**.
4. Configure **networking, encryption, tags**, and **review + create.**

Azure CLI

AZ STORAGE ACCOUNT create \

—name mystorageacct \

—resource-group myresourcegroup \

—location uksouth \

—sku Standard_LRS \

—kind StorageV2 \

—access-tier Hot

This command creates a GPv2 storage account with standard performance and locally redundant storage.

Storage Replication Options

REPLICATION PROVIDES data redundancy to ensure durability and availability.

Replication Type	Description
LRS (Locally Redundant Storage)	Copies data synchronously within a single data center.
ZRS (Zone-Redundant Storage)	Synchronously replicates across multiple zones in a region.
GRS (Geo-Redundant Storage)	Asynchronously replicates to a secondary region (read-access optional).
RA-GRS (Read-Access GRS)	Adds read access to the secondary GRS region.
GZRS / RA-GZRS	Combines ZRS and GRS for geo-zone redundancy with read access.

Replication choice affects cost, durability, and recovery capabilities. For critical workloads, **GZRS** or **RA-GZRS** is recommended.

Configuring Storage Account Features

Encryption

ALL STORAGE ACCOUNTS are encrypted at rest using Microsoft-managed keys by default. You can also use:

- **Customer-managed keys** in Azure Key Vault.
- **Double encryption** for highly sensitive data.

Enable encryption with customer-managed keys via portal or CLI:

az storage account update \

—name mystorageacct \

—resource-group myresourcegroup \

—encryption-key-source Microsoft.Keyvault \

—encryption-key-vault-properties key-name=mykey key-vault-uri=https://myvault.vault.azure.net

Networking and Firewalls

YOU CAN RESTRICT ACCESS to your storage account:

- Allow traffic only from specific **virtual networks** or **IP ranges**.
- Use **private endpoints** for secure access via private IP.

az storage account network-rule add \

—resource-group myresourcegroup \

—account-name mystorageacct \

—ip-address 203.0.113.5

Enable private endpoint:

az network private-endpoint create \

—name myPrivateEndpoint \

—resource-group myresourcegroup \

—vnet-name myVnet \

—subnet mySubnet \

—private-connection-resource-id <storage-account-id> \

—group-id blob

Azure Storage Resource Providers and API Versioning

STORAGE ACCOUNTS ARE managed through the resource provider:

- **Microsoft.Storage**

Ensure it's registered:

az provider register—namespace Microsoft.Storage

Versioning allows control over API compatibility for advanced configurations and automation scenarios.

Access Control and RBAC

STORAGE ACCOUNTS SUPPORT both:

- **Azure RBAC**: Controls access at the Azure resource level.
- **Shared Access Signatures (SAS)**: Grants time-limited, granular access.

To grant Reader role to a user:

az role assignment create \

—assignee user@domain.com \

—role "Storage Blob Data Reader" \

—scope /subscriptions/xxx/resourceGroups/xxx/providers/Microsoft.Storage/storageAccounts/mystorageacct

SAS Example:

az storage container generate-sas \

—account-name mystorageacct \

—name mycontainer \

—permissions r \

—expiry 2025-12-31T23:59Z \

—output tsv

Monitoring and Diagnostics

ENABLE DIAGNOSTICS and send logs to Log Analytics, Event Hub, or Storage Account for retention and analysis.

az monitor diagnostic-settings create \

—resource "/subscriptions/.../storageAccounts/mystorageacct" \

—workspace "/subscriptions/.../resourceGroups/rg/providers/Microsoft.OperationalInsights/workspaces/logs-ws" \

—name "storageDiag" \

—logs '[{"category": "StorageRead", "enabled": true}]'

Monitor metrics such as:

- Capacity
- Transactions
- Latency
- Egress and ingress traffic

Set alerts to be notified of anomalies or failures.

Naming Rules and Limits

- Names must be globally unique and 3–24 characters (lowercase letters and numbers only).
- Storage account limits:

  ○ Up to 5000 accounts per region per subscription (soft limit).

  ○ Max 100 PB per subscription (via support request).

  ○ Max throughput: depends on SKU and performance tier.

Cost Considerations

COSTS DEPEND ON:

- Type of storage account (standard/premium)

- Data redundancy option
- Access tier (hot/cool/archive)
- Transactions (read/write/delete)
- Outbound data transfers (egress)

Use the **Azure Pricing Calculator** to estimate costs:

https://azure.microsoft.com/en-us/pricing/calculator/

Set budgets and alerts:

```
az consumption budget create \
—amount 100 \
—time-grain monthly \
—name "StorageBudget" \
—resource-group "myresourcegroup" \
—category cost
```

Common Use Cases

Use Case	Recommended Configuration
Hosting a static website	GPv2 + Blob Storage + Static Website enabled
File shares for VMs	FileStorage or GPv2 + Azure Files
Cold archive for compliance	GPv2 + Blob Storage with Archive access tier
High-performance database logs	Premium + BlockBlobStorage or FileStorage
Cross-region DR	GPv2 + RA-GRS or RA-GZRS

Summary

CREATING AND CONFIGURING Azure Storage Accounts is a foundational skill for Azure Administrators. With the right configurations for performance, replication, security, and cost, storage accounts can serve diverse workloads—ranging from critical databases and backups to static web hosting and long-term archival. By using tools like the Azure CLI, monitoring logs, and applying access controls, administrators can ensure resilient, secure, and optimized storage solutions that align with enterprise needs.

Azure Blob Storage: Security, Tiers, and Lifecycle

AZURE BLOB STORAGE is Microsoft's object storage solution for the cloud, designed to store massive amounts of unstructured data. It supports a broad range of applications including web and mobile content delivery, backup and restore, disaster recovery, data archiving, analytics, and even machine learning. Understanding how to implement security best practices, manage access tiers, and configure data lifecycle policies is essential for maximizing both the performance and cost-efficiency of Blob Storage.

What is Blob Storage?

BLOB STANDS FOR **Binary Large Object**, and Azure Blob Storage is optimized for storing text or binary data such as images, video, documents, backups, and logs. It is highly scalable, supports REST APIs, and is deeply integrated with other Azure services.

Blob Storage is organized into:

- **Storage Account**
  - **Container** (like folders)
    - **Blobs** (actual files or objects)

There are three types of blobs:

Blob Type	Description
Block Blobs	Best for files, media, and documents; optimized for streaming.
Append Blobs	Ideal for log files and audit trails; optimized for append-only.
Page Blobs	Used by Azure VMs for disks; optimized for random read/write.

Security and Access Control

SECURITY IS A CRITICAL aspect of managing Blob Storage. Azure provides multiple layers of protection:

Authentication Options

1. **Azure Active Directory (Azure AD)**

○ Recommended for enterprise scenarios.

○ Use role-based access control (RBAC) to assign roles like:

▪ Storage Blob Data Reader

▪ Storage Blob Data Contributor

○ Supports managed identities and service principals.

2. **Shared Access Signatures (SAS)**

○ Provide time-bound, scoped access to blobs or containers.

○ Useful for temporary sharing or application-level access.

3. **Access Keys**

○ Two keys are provided per account.

○ Should be rotated regularly and stored in Azure Key Vault.

EXAMPLE: ASSIGNING RBAC access

az role assignment create \

—assignee user@domain.com \

—role "Storage Blob Data Contributor" \

—scope "/subscriptions/xxxx/resourceGroups/rg/providers/Microsoft.Storage/storageAccounts/myblobstorage"

Network Security

- **Firewalls and Virtual Networks**: Restrict access to specific IPs or VNets.
- **Private Endpoints**: Enable access to blob data through a private IP within your VNet.

AZ STORAGE ACCOUNT network-rule add \

—account-name myblobstorage \

—ip-address 203.0.113.0

Encryption

- **At Rest**:
  - Default encryption using Microsoft-managed keys.
  - Option for customer-managed keys via Key Vault.
  - Support for double encryption.
- **In Transit**:
  - Enforced via HTTPS endpoints.
  - HTTPS-only access can be enforced using account-level setting:

AZ STORAGE ACCOUNT update \

—name myblobstorage \

—https-only true

Access Tiers

BLOB STORAGE SUPPORTS different access tiers that help manage costs based on data access frequency.

Tier	Use Case	Retrieval Latency	Storage Cost	Access Cost
Hot	Active data in frequent use	Low	High	Low
Cool	Infrequent access (30+ days)	Medium	Lower	Higher
Archive	Rare access (180+ days)	High (hours)	Lowest	Highest

You can set the tier at the time of upload or update it later.

az storage blob upload \

—container-name mycontainer \

—file myfile.txt \

—name myfile.txt \

—account-name myblobstorage \

—tier Cool

To change the tier of an existing blob:

az storage blob set-tier \

—container-name mycontainer \

—name myfile.txt \

—tier Archive

Note: Accessing archive-tier blobs requires rehydration, which can take hours.

Containers and Blob Properties

Creating Containers

CONTAINERS ARE CREATED within storage accounts and act as directories for blobs.

az storage container create \

—name mycontainer \

—account-name myblobstorage \

—public-access off

You can configure public access levels:

- off: No anonymous access.
- blob: Public read access for blobs only.
- container: Public read access for blobs and container metadata.

Blob Properties and Metadata

EACH BLOB SUPPORTS:

- **Metadata**: Custom name-value pairs (e.g., department, owner).
- **Tags**: Indexable key-value pairs for search and filtering.
- **Properties**: Size, content type, encryption status, etc.

Adding metadata:

```
az storage blob metadata update \
—container-name mycontainer \
—name myfile.txt \
—metadata department=finance owner=jdoe
```

Lifecycle Management Policies

TO OPTIMIZE STORAGE usage and control costs, you can configure **lifecycle management** rules to automate blob tier transitions and deletion.

Use cases include:

- Moving blobs to **Cool** tier after 30 days of inactivity.
- Deleting blobs from **Archive** tier after 365 days.
- Deleting **uncommitted blobs** older than 7 days.

Sample policy:

```
{
"rules": [
```

```
{
"enabled": true,
"name": "tierPolicy",
"type": "Lifecycle",
"definition": {
"filters": {
"blobTypes": [ "blockBlob" ],
"prefixMatch": [ "logs/" ]
},
"actions": {
"baseBlob": {
"tierToCool": {
"daysAfterModificationGreaterThan": 30
},
"tierToArchive": {
"daysAfterModificationGreaterThan": 90
},
"delete": {
"daysAfterModificationGreaterThan": 365
}
```

}

}

}

}

]

}

Enable via CLI:

az storage account management-policy create \

—account-name myblobstorage \

—resource-group rg \

—policy @lifecycle.json

Monitoring and Logging

AZURE MONITOR AND DIAGNOSTIC Settings enable visibility into blob operations.

Enable diagnostic settings:

az monitor diagnostic-settings create \

—resource "/subscriptions/xxx/resourceGroups/rg/providers/Microsoft.Storage/storageAccounts/myblobstorage" \

—workspace "/subscriptions/xxx/resourceGroups/logs-rg/providers/Microsoft.OperationalInsights/workspaces/mylogs" \

—name "blobDiagnostics" \

—logs '[{"category": "StorageRead", "enabled": true}]'

Track metrics such as:

- Number of read/write/delete operations
- Latency
- Capacity utilization

These insights help identify performance bottlenecks or unauthorized access.

Static Website Hosting with Blob Storage

BLOB STORAGE SUPPORTS static website hosting for single-page apps, documentation, and landing pages.

Steps:

1. Enable static website hosting:

az storage blob service-properties update \

—account-name myblobstorage \

—static-website \

—index-document index.html \

—error-document 404.html

1. Upload content to the $web container.
2. Access via https://<account>.z13.web.core.windows.net

This is a highly cost-effective way to serve static content.

Integration with Azure Services

BLOB STORAGE IS DEEPLY integrated with many Azure services:

Service	Integration Purpose
Azure Data Factory	Source/destination for data pipelines
Azure Synapse Analytics	Data lake for analytics workloads
Azure Functions	Event-driven processing of blob events
Azure Logic Apps	Automated workflows based on blob actions
Azure Backup	Backup vaults use blob storage for long-term retention

Blob events (e.g., blob created/deleted) can trigger **Event Grid**, **Functions**, or **Logic Apps** for automation.

Best Practices

- **Use RBAC for access control** over access keys whenever possible.

ENABLE SOFT DELETE for accidental recovery:

az storage blob service-properties update \

—account-name myblobstorage \

—enable-delete-retention true \

—delete-retention-days 7

-

- **Enable versioning** to track changes to blobs.

- Use **Cool/Archive tiers** for infrequent access data.
- **Monitor access** with Azure Monitor and secure sensitive data using encryption and private endpoints.
- **Implement lifecycle rules** to automate transitions and deletion of stale data.
- Use **naming conventions** and metadata for manageability and automation.

Summary

AZURE BLOB STORAGE is a powerful and flexible object storage platform that can handle a wide array of data storage needs. By configuring appropriate security controls, selecting the right access tiers, and implementing lifecycle management policies, Azure Administrators can ensure that their blob storage deployments are secure, scalable, and cost-effective. Mastery of Blob Storage is essential for administrators who are managing data at scale in the cloud.

File Shares and Azure Files

AZURE FILES IS A MANAGED file share service in the cloud that enables users and applications to mount SMB and NFS shares directly into Azure virtual machines or from on-premises systems. With full support for the Server Message Block (SMB) protocol and Network File System (NFS), Azure Files offers a powerful solution for lift-and-shift scenarios, shared application data, configuration management, and hybrid connectivity.

Azure Files is part of the broader Azure Storage account ecosystem and delivers shared access, access control, high availability, and native integration with Azure Backup and Azure File Sync. This section explores the creation, configuration, security, and real-world use of Azure Files.

What is Azure Files?

AZURE FILES ALLOWS for fully managed file shares in the cloud that can be mounted simultaneously by cloud or on-premises deployments. Azure file shares are deployed within **storage accounts**, and support standard file system operations like read, write, delete, and list.

Two protocols are supported:

- **SMB (Server Message Block)**: Common in Windows environments. Supported by Windows, macOS, and Linux.
- **NFS (Network File System)**: Linux/Unix-based file sharing.

Azure Files is suitable for:

- Centralized configuration storage for distributed applications
- Shared directories for Azure VMs
- Hosting profiles for Windows Virtual Desktop
- On-premises integration via Azure File Sync
- Backup storage for databases or applications

Tiers and Performance Options

AZURE FILES SUPPORTS two performance tiers:

Tier	Description	Use Cases
Standard	Backed by HDDs, available in general-purpose v2 accounts	General purpose file shares
Premium	Backed by SSDs, available in FileStorage accounts	High IOPS and throughput for heavy usage

Feature	Standard (Transaction Optimized)	Premium (FileStorage)
Max Capacity per Share	100 TiB	100 TiB
Throughput	Up to 60 MiB/s	Up to 1000 MiB/s
IOPS	~1000 per share	100,000+ per share (scale based)
Protocols Supported	SMB, NFS	SMB

You can also configure **hot** and **cool** access tiers for standard file shares to optimize cost.

Creating Azure File Shares

Using Azure Portal

1. Navigate to **Storage Accounts → myaccount → File Shares**.
2. Click + **File Share.**
3. Name the share, specify quota, select tier, and create.

Using Azure CLI

AZ STORAGE SHARE CREATE \

—name myfileshare \

—account-name mystorageacct \

—quota 100 \

—access-tier TransactionOptimized

For premium shares:

az storage share create \

—name mypremiumshare \

—account-name mystorageacct \

—quota 5120 \

—enabled-protocols SMB \

—account-kind FileStorage

You can retrieve the share's connection string:

az storage account keys list \

—account-name mystorageacct \

—query "[0].value" \

—output tsv

Mounting Azure File Shares

Windows (SMB)

```
NET USE Z: \\MYSTORAGEACCT.file.core.windows.net\
myfileshare /u:mystorageacct <storage-key>
```

Linux (SMB)

```
SUDO MOUNT -T CIFS //mystorageacct.file.core.windows.net/
myfileshare /mnt/myfileshare \

-o
vers=3.0,username=mystorageacct,password=<storage-key>,dir_mode=0
```

Linux (NFS – Premium only)

```
SUDO MOUNT -T NFS
MYSTORAGEACCT.file.core.windows.net:/myfileshare /mnt/
myfileshare
```

Access Control and Security

AZURE FILES SUPPORTS multiple security mechanisms:

Authentication Options

1. **Storage Account Keys**

   ○ Default access mechanism using primary or secondary key.

   ○ Suitable for legacy and programmatic access.

2. **Shared Access Signatures (SAS)**

   ○ Grant scoped, time-bound access to clients or services.

3. **Azure Active Directory Domain Services (Azure AD DS)**

   ○ Enables domain-joined authentication for SMB shares.

4. **Azure AD Kerberos (preview)**

   ○ Enables domainless authentication using Azure AD identity.

Configuring Azure AD DS Authentication

- Join the storage account to the domain:

```
AZ STORAGE ACCOUNT update \
—name mystorageacct \
—resource-group rg \
—enable-files-aadds true
```

- Assign permissions via Azure role Storage File Data SMB Share Contributor.

Network Security

- Use **firewalls and virtual networks** to restrict access.
- For private connectivity, configure **private endpoints**.

- Enforce **HTTPS-only** access for secure transmission.

AZ STORAGE ACCOUNT update \

—name mystorageacct \

—https-only true

Azure File Sync

AZURE FILE SYNC TRANSFORMS an Azure file share into a cloud-based extension of your on-premises file server. It enables centralized file share hosting with caching and synchronization across distributed environments.

Key Benefits:

- Centralized cloud storage with local caching
- Multi-site sync and tiering
- Backup and DR support
- Integration with Windows Server File System

Setup Steps:

1. Create a file share in Azure.
2. Deploy Azure File Sync agent on your on-prem Windows Server.
3. Register the server with Azure File Sync.
4. Create a **Sync Group** and add endpoints (cloud and on-prem).
5. Enable **cloud tiering** to offload cold files and save local disk space.

CLOUD TIERING CAN BE configured by file age, size, or access patterns.

Backup and Restore

AZURE FILES INTEGRATES natively with Azure Backup to provide file share protection.

Enabling Backup:

1. Navigate to **Recovery Services Vault → Backup**.
2. Choose **Azure File Share** as the workload type.
3. Select storage account and share.
4. Define backup policy (frequency, retention).
5. Monitor job status and alerts.

YOU CAN ALSO USE POWERSHELL or CLI for backup automation.

Restore options include:

- Individual files or directories
- Entire share to original or alternate location
- Point-in-time restore

Azure Backup supports **soft delete** for file shares, allowing recovery of deleted shares for up to 14 days.

Enable soft delete:

az storage account file-service-properties update \

—account-name mystorageacct \

—enable-delete-retention true \

—delete-retention-days 14

Monitoring and Metrics

MONITORING IS AVAILABLE through Azure Monitor and can be configured to send data to:

- Log Analytics workspace
- Event Hub
- Storage Account (for archival)

Metrics include:

- Availability
- IOPS and throughput
- Capacity utilization
- Read/write latency

Enable diagnostic settings:

az monitor diagnostic-settings create \

—name "fileshare-logs" \

—resource "/subscriptions/xxx/resourceGroups/rg/providers/Microsoft.Storage/storageAccounts/mystorageacct" \

—workspace "/subscriptions/xxx/resourceGroups/logs-rg/providers/Microsoft.OperationalInsights/workspaces/mylogs" \

—logs '[{"category": "FileShare", "enabled": true}]'

Set alerts for abnormal performance or high usage:

- Share nearing quota
- Excessive failed mount attempts
- Latency thresholds exceeded

Best Practices

- Use **premium shares** for IOPS-intensive workloads.
- Enable **Azure AD DS** or **Kerberos auth** for secure, role-based access.
- Implement **Azure File Sync** for hybrid file server scenarios.
- Regularly **rotate access keys** and prefer identity-based access.
- Use **soft delete** and **backup policies** to protect critical data.
- Apply **tags** and **naming standards** to organize shares efficiently.
- Use **lifecycle management** on standard shares for archival and cost control.

Common Use Cases

Use Case	Recommended Approach
App configuration file storage	Standard tier SMB shares
Windows Virtual Desktop profiles	Premium tier SMB with AD DS integration
Hybrid file servers	Azure File Sync with cloud tiering
Shared logs or output directories	NFS shares on premium accounts
Database backups and archival	Cool tier standard shares with backup policies

Summary

AZURE FILES ENABLES organizations to build highly available, secure, and scalable file sharing solutions without maintaining traditional file servers. From SMB and NFS protocol support to hybrid sync capabilities, role-based access control, and native backup integration, Azure Files delivers the enterprise-grade functionality needed for modern cloud and hybrid infrastructures. By mastering Azure Files, administrators ensure reliable access to shared resources while optimizing performance, security, and cost-efficiency.

Data Protection and Redundancy Options

ENSURING DATA PROTECTION and availability is a core responsibility of Azure Administrators. Microsoft Azure offers a comprehensive set of built-in redundancy options and protection features to safeguard data against hardware failures, network outages, accidental deletions, and natural disasters. These options are integrated across all major Azure Storage services, especially Azure Blob, File, Queue, and Table Storage.

In this section, we will explore the mechanisms Azure provides to maintain data durability, implement backup and restore strategies, replicate data across regions, recover from deletion or corruption, and ensure regulatory compliance.

Storage Redundancy Overview

REDUNDANCY ENSURES that data remains available and durable in the event of hardware or datacenter failure. Azure Storage replicates data automatically and offers several redundancy configurations.

Local Redundant Storage (LRS)

- **Description**: Replicates data **three times** within a single physical location (datacenter).
- **Durability**: 11 nines (99.999999999%) over a given year.
- **Use Case**: Cost-effective, non-critical data that can tolerate datacenter loss.

Zone-Redundant Storage (ZRS)

- **Description**: Replicates synchronously across **three availability zones** in a region.
- **Durability**: High availability for read and write operations.
- **Use Case**: Production workloads requiring high availability within a region.

Geo-Redundant Storage (GRS)

- **Description**: Replicates data **asynchronously** to a secondary geographic region (hundreds of miles away).
- **Durability**: Up to 16 nines of durability by storing 6 copies (3 primary, 3 secondary).
- **Use Case**: Disaster recovery scenarios, compliance with regional replication mandates.

Read-Access GRS (RA-GRS)

- **Adds**: Read access to the secondary endpoint.
- **Use Case**: Allows read-only operations during primary region outages.

Geo-Zone-Redundant Storage (GZRS) / Read-Access GZRS (RA-GZRS)

- **Description**: Combines the benefits of ZRS and GRS.
- **Replicates**: Across zones in primary and asynchronously to a secondary region.
- **Use Case**: Mission-critical workloads needing maximum availability and geographic durability.

Choosing the Right Redundancy Option

Redundancy Option	Region Scope	Zones Used	Geo-Replication	Read Access in DR	Cost	Best For
LRS	Single	No	No	No	Low	Backups, test environments
ZRS	Regional	Yes	No	No	Medium	Production apps with HA
GRS	Cross-Region	No	Yes	No	Higher	DR-compliant workloads
RA-GRS	Cross-Region	No	Yes	Yes	Higher	Critical apps with read-failover
GZRS	Cross-Region	Yes	Yes	No	Highest	Apps needing zone+geo redundancy
RA-GZRS	Cross-Region	Yes	Yes	Yes	Highest	Premium DR and availability needs

CHOOSE BASED ON DATA criticality, SLA requirements, cost sensitivity, and compliance.

Enabling and Configuring Redundancy

WHEN CREATING A STORAGE account, redundancy is selected in the replication options:

```
az storage account create \
—name mystorageacct \
—resource-group myresourcegroup \
—location uksouth \
—sku Standard_GRS \
—kind StorageV2
```

To switch redundancy later (note: some changes are not reversible):

```
az storage account update \
—name mystorageacct \
—sku Standard_LRS
```

Be cautious—downgrading from geo-redundant to local could result in data loss in case of regional outage.

Data Protection Features

Soft Delete for Blobs

PROTECTS BLOBS FROM accidental or malicious deletion.

- Retains deleted blobs for a defined period (1-365 days).
- Allows restoration without additional configuration.

Enable soft delete:

```
az storage blob service-properties update \
—account-name mystorageacct \
```

—enable-delete-retention true \

—delete-retention-days 14

Soft Delete for File Shares

SIMILAR TO BLOB SOFT delete, applicable to Azure Files.

az storage account file-service-properties update \

—account-name mystorageacct \

—enable-delete-retention true \

—delete-retention-days 7

Container and Share Snapshots

- Snapshots capture read-only, point-in-time versions of blobs or file shares.
- Useful for quick restore scenarios or data audits.

CREATE A BLOB SNAPSHOT:

az storage blob snapshot create \

—account-name mystorageacct \

—container-name mycontainer \

—name myblob.txt

Versioning

AUTOMATIC VERSION CREATION on blob modifications:

az storage blob service-properties update \

—account-name mystorageacct \

—enable-versioning true

You can retrieve or delete specific versions using—version-id.

Azure Backup Integration

AZURE BACKUP SUPPORTS:

- Azure Blob (preview for selected tiers)
- Azure File shares
- Azure Disks
- SQL databases on Azure VMs

To configure:

1. Create a **Recovery Services Vault**.
2. Register storage account or VM.
3. Define backup policies.
4. Enable backup and schedule.

Backup CLI for Azure Files:

az backup protection enable-for-azurefileshare \

—vault-name myvault \

—resource-group rg \

—storage-account mystorageacct \

—azure-file-share myshare \

—policy-name DailyPolicy

Azure Site Recovery

AZURE SITE RECOVERY (ASR) provides full disaster recovery capabilities. While ASR is primarily used for VMs, it works in tandem with storage redundancy to offer cross-region failover.

Steps:

1. Enable replication on the source VM.
2. Select target region and storage.
3. Configure replication policy.
4. Test failover.

For storage-native redundancy, this adds value only in VM-level replication and orchestration of full app recovery.

Monitoring and Auditing Redundancy and Protection

USE AZURE MONITOR, Activity Logs, and Diagnostic Settings to track:

- Replication changes
- Blob deletions and recoveries
- Backup and snapshot operations
- Retention policy updates

Configure diagnostic logs:

```
az monitor diagnostic-settings create \
—resource "/subscriptions/xxx/resourceGroups/rg/providers/Microsoft.Storage/storageAccounts/mystorageacct" \
—workspace "/subscriptions/xxx/resourceGroups/logs-rg/providers/Microsoft.OperationalInsights/workspaces/mylogs" \
—logs '[{"category": "StorageDelete", "enabled": true}]'
```

Set alerts for deletion events or replication downgrades.

Regulatory Compliance and Retention

AZURE'S STORAGE REDUNDANCY and protection mechanisms can help meet compliance requirements such as:

- **GDPR**: Soft delete and region-restricted storage.
- **HIPAA**: Durable storage for PHI with audit logs.
- **ISO 27001**: Secure storage with regional replication and encryption.
- **SOC 1/2/3**: System availability and data integrity commitments.

Use **immutability policies** (legal hold, time-based retention) to protect data against alteration:

```
az storage container immutability-policy create \
—container-name logs \
—account-name mystorageacct \
—period 365
```

Best Practices

- **Always use RA-GRS or GZRS** for critical business data.
- **Enable soft delete and versioning** to protect against data loss.
- **Use snapshots** before critical updates or deployments.
- **Automate backup and policy enforcement** using scripts or ARM templates.
- **Combine redundancy with monitoring** to detect and respond to events.
- **Train teams** on how to recover deleted data using CLI and portal tools.
- **Document data protection policies** and store them centrally.

Summary

AZURE'S DATA PROTECTION and redundancy offerings provide comprehensive options to maintain high availability, durability, and recoverability. By leveraging LRS, ZRS, GRS, and advanced features like soft delete, snapshots, backup integration, and geo-redundant replication, Azure Administrators can build resilient cloud architectures that safeguard against both accidental loss and systemic failure. A robust data protection strategy is not only essential for operational continuity but also a cornerstone of regulatory compliance and organizational trust.

Import/Export and Azure Data Box

IN THE AGE OF PETABYTE-scale data, organizations often face the challenge of transferring large volumes of data into or out of the cloud. While Azure provides powerful network-based tools like AzCopy, Azure Data Factory, and Azure Storage Explorer, these solutions may be impractical when bandwidth constraints, cost limitations, or time sensitivity are involved. To address such needs, Microsoft Azure offers the **Import/Export Service** and **Azure Data Box**, purpose-built for secure, high-capacity offline data transfer.

This section covers these tools in depth, helping Azure Administrators understand when and how to use them for efficient large-scale data ingestion, migration, disaster recovery, and data export scenarios.

Understanding Azure Import/Export and Data Box

Feature	Azure Import/ Export	Azure Data Box
Transport Medium	User-provided hard drives	Microsoft-provided secure appliances
Max Capacity	Limited by number of drives	40 TB to 1 PB+ depending on model
Online Connectivity	None	Some models support online transfer
Target Services	Azure Blob or File Storage	Azure Storage, Azure Stack, etc.
Encryption Required	Yes	Built-in (AES 256-bit)
Primary Use Case	Small to medium datasets	Terabyte-scale or petabyte-scale

BOTH OPTIONS ARE ESPECIALLY useful for:

- Initial cloud migrations
- Bulk ingestion of video/media content
- Data center evacuations
- Disaster recovery from offline backups
- Government or air-gapped transfers

Azure Import/Export Service

THE AZURE IMPORT/EXPORT Service enables data transfer to and from Azure using **BitLocker-encrypted** hard drives shipped by the user. This service is cost-effective and suitable for smaller data sets (<10 TB).

Supported Scenarios

- Importing data into Azure Blob Storage
- Exporting data from Azure Storage to external drives

Requirements

- SATA II/III 2.5" or 3.5" external drives
- NTFS file system format
- BitLocker encryption

- Import/export jobs created via Azure Portal or PowerShell

Steps for Importing Data

Step 1: Prepare the Drives

- Format the drives with NTFS.
- Encrypt using BitLocker with a strong key.

ENABLE-BITLOCKER -MOUNTPOINT "E:" -EncryptionMethod XtsAes256 -PasswordProtector

Step 2: Install WAImportExport Tool

- Download from the Microsoft website.
- Use the tool to prepare and map files.

WAIMPORTEXPORT.EXE PrepImport /sk:<storagekey> /id:job123 /DriveLetter:E /srcdir:C:\data

Step 3: Create Import Job in Azure

NEW-AZIMPORTEXPORTJOB `

-StorageAccountName "mystorageacct" `

-ResourceGroupName "rg" `

-Location "uksouth" `

-JobName "myimportjob" `

-DriveList @(@{ DriveId = "9J27B3"; BitLockerKey = "xxxxx" }) `

-ReturnAddress @{ RecipientName = "IT Admin"; StreetAddress1 = "1 Azure Way"; CountryOrRegion = "UK" }

Step 4: Ship Drives

SEND DRIVES TO THE Microsoft data center address listed in your job. Tracking info is uploaded in the portal.

Step 5: Job Completion

AZURE INGESTS THE DATA and notifies you. You can then delete the job and reuse the drives.

Steps for Exporting Data

1. Create an export job in the portal.
2. Azure copies selected blobs to BitLocker-encrypted drives.
3. Microsoft ships drives to your physical location.
4. You decrypt and copy the data locally.

Azure Data Box

AZURE DATA BOX IS A family of physical appliances managed by Microsoft and shipped to your location for large data transfers. It offers higher capacity, enhanced security, and better reliability than Import/Export.

Models and Specifications

Device	Capacity	Use Case
Data Box	Up to 80 TB	Mid-size migration, data center moves
Data Box Disk	8 TB each (up to 35 TB)	Smaller workloads, branch offices
Data Box Heavy	Up to 1 PB	Massive-scale lift-and-shift projects
Data Box Gateway	Virtual appliance	Continuous online ingestion (NFS/SMB)

ALL MODELS FEATURE **AES 256-bit encryption**, **tamper-resistant hardware**, **secure chain of custody**, and are **compliant with many industry standards** (HIPAA, ISO, GDPR).

Workflow for Using Azure Data Box

Step 1: Order and Provision

CREATE AN ORDER VIA the Azure Portal:

```
az databox job create \
—name databoxjob01 \
—resource-group rg \
—location uksouth \
—sku Standard \
—transfer-type ImportToAzure \
—storage-account mystorageacct
```

Specify shipping and contact details.

Step 2: Receive and Connect

- Connect Data Box to your network via Ethernet.
- Access the local UI over HTTPS.
- Mount the shares using SMB (Windows/Linux).

Step 3: Copy Data

USE TOOLS LIKE **Robocopy**, **AzCopy**, or **Data Box SDK** to copy files:

robocopy D:\data \\<DataBoxIPAddress>\sharedfolder /E

Monitor logs for data transfer validation.

Step 4: Return and Upload

- Seal the device (tamper seal required).
- Ship back using included return label.
- Microsoft uploads data to your designated storage account.

JOB STATUS AND LOGS are accessible via the Azure Portal.

Data Box Gateway (Online Mode)

DATA BOX GATEWAY ACTS as a network appliance that continuously transfers on-premises data to Azure Blob or File Storage. Ideal for hybrid or edge scenarios.

- Runs as a VM on Hyper-V or VMware
- Connects via SMB/NFS shares
- Buffered uploads during connectivity loss

Use it for:

- Daily ingestion of logs or backups
- Gradual cloud migration
- Edge-to-cloud pipelines

Security and Compliance

AZURE ENSURES SECURE data transport by:

- Encrypting all data at rest and in transit.
- Validating device integrity through tamper-proof seals.
- Wiping devices after upload using NIST-compliant procedures.
- Maintaining full tracking logs and chain-of-custody records.

Administrators can download audit logs and transfer manifests from the Azure Portal.

Monitoring and Troubleshooting

MONITOR JOB STATUS, capacity usage, and error rates via:

- Azure Portal
- Data Box local UI
- Log exports (CSV, JSON)
- Alerts (email, SMS) for job state transitions

Example: Check Data Box job status:

az databox job show—name databoxjob01—resource-group rg

Common issues:

- Slow copy rates (network bottlenecks, small file count)
- Device not detected (driver or firmware mismatch)
- Job delays (customs clearance or incomplete documentation)

Best Practices

- Pre-check with **Data Box Planner** to estimate time and model.
- Use **Azure AzCopy** or **Robocopy** for optimized transfer.

- Validate data before sealing device.
- Tag your import/export data for traceability.
- Enable logging during transfers for audit purposes.
- Always ensure **physical security** when devices are onsite.

Summary

AZURE IMPORT/EXPORT and Data Box services address one of the biggest challenges in cloud adoption: large-scale data transfer. Whether you're moving terabytes of data to start a migration or exporting sensitive datasets for compliance audits, these services offer scalable, secure, and cost-efficient pathways for offline data logistics. As an Azure Administrator, knowing when and how to use these tools equips you to support complex migration, hybrid cloud, and data compliance initiatives with confidence.

Chapter 4: Deploying and Managing Azure Compute Resources

Virtual Machines: Creation and Configuration

AZURE VIRTUAL MACHINES (VMs) are one of the core offerings in Microsoft Azure's Infrastructure-as-a-Service (IaaS) portfolio. They provide on-demand, scalable computing resources that you can use for a wide range of purposes—from hosting legacy applications to supporting modern containerized workloads. As an Azure Administrator, the ability to create, configure, manage, and secure VMs is fundamental to supporting your organization's cloud operations.

Understanding Azure Virtual Machines

AN AZURE VM IS A VIRTUALIZED compute environment hosted in Microsoft's data centers. It includes:

- **CPU and memory** specifications based on size and family
- **OS disk** and optional **data disks**
- **Networking interface** (NIC) with public or private IPs
- **Operating system** (Windows or Linux)
- **Management agents** for updates, monitoring, and backups

Azure VMs support custom images, shared images, generalized and specialized VHDs, and can be deployed individually or as part of a scale set or availability set.

VM Sizing and Series

AZURE OFFERS A WIDE range of VM sizes optimized for various workloads. Some common VM series:

Series	Description	Use Case
B	Burstable performance	Dev/test, low-traffic workloads
D	General purpose	Web servers, apps, databases
E	Memory optimized	In-memory databases
F	Compute optimized	Batch processing, game servers
M	High memory (up to 3.8 TB RAM)	SAP HANA, large-scale analytics
NV/NC	GPU-based VMs	AI/ML, graphics rendering

Choose the smallest size that meets your performance needs to optimize costs.

Creating a VM

Azure Portal

1. Navigate to **Virtual Machines → Create.**
2. Select **Resource Group**, **VM name**, and **Region**.
3. Choose an OS image (e.g., Ubuntu 22.04, Windows Server 2022).
4. Select a VM size (e.g., D2s_v3).

5. Configure administrator credentials and networking.
6. Optionally enable monitoring, backup, and security options.
7. Review and deploy.

Azure CLI

AZ VM CREATE \

—name myvm \

—resource-group myresourcegroup \

—image UbuntuLTS \

—admin-username azureuser \

—generate-ssh-keys \

—size Standard_D2s_v3 \

—location uksouth

To create a Windows VM:

az vm create \

—resource-group myresourcegroup \

—name mywinvm \

—image Win2019Datacenter \

—admin-username azureadmin \

—admin-password "ComplexP@ssw0rd!"

Configuring Disks

AZURE VMS SUPPORT:

- **OS Disk**: Required, contains the operating system.
- **Temporary Disk**: Ephemeral local storage (D:\ on Windows).
- **Data Disks**: Optional, used for app and data storage.

Types of managed disks:

Type	Performance	Use Case
Standard HDD	Cost-effective, basic I/O	Test/dev, infrequent access
Standard SSD	Balanced performance/ cost	Web servers, small databases
Premium SSD	High performance	Production, latency-sensitive
Ultra Disk	Max IOPS and throughput	High-performance databases

To attach a data disk:

```
az vm disk attach \
—resource-group myresourcegroup \
—vm-name myvm \
—name datadisk1 \
—size-gb 128
```

Networking Configuration

EACH VM IS CONNECTED to:

- A **Virtual Network (VNet)** and **subnet**
- A **Network Interface (NIC)**
- Optionally, a **public IP address**
- **Network Security Group (NSG)** to control inbound/ outbound traffic

To allow SSH (port 22) or RDP (port 3389), define NSG rules:

az vm open-port \

—port 22 \

—resource-group myresourcegroup \

—name myvm

Configure internal-only VMs by disabling the public IP.

OS Configuration

AFTER PROVISIONING, configure the VM:

- Install updates and security patches
- Enable auto-shutdown and time zone settings
- Configure swap space or page files (especially on Linux)
- Install desired applications or services

You can connect via:

- **SSH (Linux)**: ssh azureuser@<public-ip>
- **RDP (Windows)**: Using the RDP file from the portal

VM Extensions and Custom Scripts

AZURE VM EXTENSIONS enable post-deployment configuration. Examples include:

- **Custom Script Extension**: Run shell scripts or PowerShell
- **Log Analytics Agent**: For monitoring and logging
- **Antimalware Extension**: Enable Microsoft Antimalware

Linux example:

```
az vm extension set \
—publisher Microsoft.Azure.Extensions \
—name CustomScript \
—resource-group myresourcegroup \
—vm-name myvm \
—settings '{"fileUris":["https://example.com/script.sh"],"commandToExecute":"sh script.sh"}'
```

Availability and Redundancy

ENSURE HIGH AVAILABILITY by using:

- **Availability Sets**: Distribute VMs across update and fault domains.
- **Availability Zones**: Deploy VMs in different physical datacenters within a region.
- **Proximity Placement Groups**: Minimize latency between VMs.

Creating an availability set:

az vm availability-set create \

—name myavailset \

—resource-group myresourcegroup \

—platform-fault-domain-count 2 \

—platform-update-domain-count 5

Use **Load Balancers** to distribute traffic among VMs in an availability set or scale set.

VM Management Tasks

Start/Stop/Restart

AZ VM START—NAME MYVM—RESOURCE-group myresourcegroup

az vm stop—name myvm—resource-group myresourcegroup

az vm restart—name myvm—resource-group myresourcegroup

Resize a VM

CHANGE VM SIZE:

az vm resize \

—resource-group myresourcegroup \

—name myvm \

—size Standard_D4s_v3

VM must be deallocated to resize.

Capture VM Image

TO REUSE A VM SETUP:

az vm deallocate—resource-group myresourcegroup—name myvm

az vm generalize—resource-group myresourcegroup—name myvm

az image create—resource-group myresourcegroup—name mycustomimage—source myvm

Use the custom image for new VMs in the portal or CLI.

Monitoring and Diagnostics

ENABLE MONITORING TO track VM performance:

- **Azure Monitor**: Metrics and alerts (CPU, disk, memory)

- **Log Analytics**: Advanced queries and logging
- **Diagnostic Settings**: Export logs to Storage, Event Hub, or Log Analytics

Enable diagnostics:

az vm diagnostics set \

—resource-group myresourcegroup \

—vm-name myvm \

—settings '{"storageUri": "https://mystorageacct.blob.core.windows.net/"}'

Configure alerts for CPU thresholds, disk saturation, or downtime events.

Security Considerations

- Use **Azure Defender for Servers** to detect threats.
- Restrict RDP/SSH access with **NSG rules** and **Just-In-Time (JIT) access.**
- Use **Azure Bastion** for secure browser-based RDP/SSH without public IPs.
- Install endpoint protection and keep OS updated.
- Apply **Disk Encryption** with Azure Key Vault (BitLocker/Linux dm-crypt).

Automation and Infrastructure as Code

AUTOMATE VM DEPLOYMENTS using:

- **ARM Templates**
- **Bicep**
- **Terraform**
- **Azure CLI Scripts**
- **Azure DevOps Pipelines**

Simple Bicep example:

```
resource vm 'Microsoft.Compute/virtualMachines@2022-11-01' =
{

name: 'myvm'

location: resourceGroup().location

properties: {

hardwareProfile: { vmSize: 'Standard_D2s_v3' }

osProfile: {

computerName: 'myvm'

adminUsername: 'azureuser'

adminPassword: 'P@ssword123!'

}

storageProfile: {
```

```
imageReference: {
publisher: 'Canonical'
offer: 'UbuntuServer'
sku: '18.04-LTS'
version: 'latest'
}
osDisk: {
createOption: 'FromImage'
}
}
networkProfile: {
networkInterfaces: [
{
id: nic.id
}
]
}
}
}
```

Best Practices

- Use availability zones or sets for HA.
- Deploy behind load balancers for scalability.
- Enable monitoring and diagnostics at deployment.
- Secure VMs using NSGs, JIT access, and Bastion.
- Keep custom images updated and version-controlled.
- Avoid using public IPs unless necessary.
- Automate builds and configuration with extensions or IaC.

Summary

AZURE VIRTUAL MACHINES are a foundational service enabling administrators to run virtualized workloads in a flexible and scalable environment. By mastering VM creation, configuration, disk management, networking, availability, monitoring, and security, Azure Administrators can design resilient compute infrastructures aligned with business goals. Whether running enterprise apps, databases, development environments, or web services, Azure VMs offer the versatility needed to support modern cloud workloads effectively.

Automating Deployment with ARM Templates

IN CLOUD ENVIRONMENTS, automation is the cornerstone of consistency, scalability, and operational efficiency. Azure Resource

Manager (ARM) templates provide a declarative way to define and deploy infrastructure and services in Azure, ensuring that environments are reproducible and version-controlled. By leveraging ARM templates, Azure Administrators can deploy complete solutions repeatedly with minimal human intervention and reduced risk of configuration drift.

This section explores the structure, syntax, deployment techniques, and best practices for using ARM templates to automate infrastructure provisioning in Azure.

What Are ARM Templates?

ARM TEMPLATES ARE JSON files that describe one or more Azure resources and their configurations. Instead of manually creating resources through the Azure Portal or CLI, ARM templates allow you to define the desired state of your infrastructure in a consistent, reusable, and automated manner.

Key benefits:

- Declarative syntax (you define *what*, not *how*)
- Reusability and modular design
- Parameterization for environment-specific inputs
- Integration with source control and CI/CD pipelines
- Idempotency (re-running the same template won't cause duplication)

ARM templates are executed by Azure Resource Manager, which validates, plans, and deploys the resources as described.

ARM Template Structure

A COMPLETE ARM TEMPLATE is composed of the following sections:

Section	Purpose
$schema	Specifies the template schema location.
contentVersion	Version identifier for the template.
parameters	Inputs provided at deployment time.
variables	Internal constants or computed values.
resources	The actual Azure resources to deploy.
outputs	Return values from the deployment (e.g., URIs, IDs).

Example minimal template:

```
{
"$schema": "https://schema.management.azure.com/schemas/2019-04-01/deploymentTemplate.json#",
"contentVersion": "1.0.0.0",
"parameters": {
"vmName": {
"type": "string"
}
},
"resources": [
{
"type": "Microsoft.Compute/virtualMachines",
```

```
"apiVersion": "2022-11-01",
"name": "[parameters('vmName')]",
"location": "[resourceGroup().location]",
"properties": {
"hardwareProfile": {
"vmSize": "Standard_D2s_v3"
},
...
}
}
]
}
```

Parameters and Variables

PARAMETERS allow templates to be dynamic and reusable. You can define default values, allowed values, and descriptions.

```
"parameters": {
"location": {
"type": "string",
"defaultValue": "uksouth",
"allowedValues": ["uksouth", "westeurope"],
```

```
"metadata": {
"description": "Location for all resources."
}
}
}
```

Variables simplify complex expressions or allow reuse:

```
"variables": {
"storageAccountName": "[concat('stg', uniqueString(resourceGroup().id))]"
}
```

Resources

THE RESOURCES ARRAY contains the definitions of all Azure components you wish to deploy, such as:

- Virtual Machines
- Network Interfaces
- Public IPs
- Virtual Networks and Subnets
- Storage Accounts
- SQL Databases
- App Services

Each resource is defined by:

- type
- apiVersion
- name
- location
- dependsOn (optional)
- properties

Example: Deploying a storage account

```
{
"type": "Microsoft.Storage/storageAccounts",
"apiVersion": "2022-09-01",
"name": "[variables('storageAccountName')]",
"location": "[parameters('location')]",
"sku": {
"name": "Standard_LRS"
},
"kind": "StorageV2",
"properties": {}
}
```

Outputs

OUTPUTS PROVIDE VALUES after the deployment completes. These can be used in automation scripts or CI/CD processes.

"outputs": {

"storageAccountEndpoint": {

"type": "string",

"value": "[reference(resourceId('Microsoft.Storage/storageAccounts', variables('storageAccountName'))).primaryEndpoints.blob]"

}

}

Deploying ARM Templates

TEMPLATES CAN BE DEPLOYED via:

Azure Portal

1. Navigate to **Deploy a custom template** in the Azure Portal.
2. Paste or upload the JSON file.
3. Provide parameter values.
4. Click **Review + create.**

Azure CLI

AZ DEPLOYMENT GROUP create \

—resource-group myrg \

—template-file azuredeploy.json \

—parameters vmName=myvm location=uksouth

PowerShell

NEW-AZRESOURCEGROUPDEPLOYMENT `

-ResourceGroupName "myrg" `

-TemplateFile "azuredeploy.json" `

-vmName "myvm"

REST API / SDKs

PROGRAMMATIC DEPLOYMENTS are also supported via the Azure REST API and SDKs for .NET, JavaScript, Python, etc.

Linked and Nested Templates

ARM SUPPORTS **linked templates**, which allow you to modularize infrastructure into reusable components hosted in external URLs.

Use case: Separate templates for VNet, VMs, and NSGs.

{

"type": "Microsoft.Resources/deployments",

"apiVersion": "2021-04-01",

"name": "linkedTemplate",

"properties": {

"mode": "Incremental",

```
"templateLink": {
"uri": "https://storageaccount.blob.core.windows.net/templates/vnet.json",
"contentVersion": "1.0.0.0"
},
"parameters": {
"location": { "value": "[parameters('location')]" }
}
}
}
```

Deployment Modes

ARM SUPPORTS TWO DEPLOYMENT modes:

- **Incremental** (default): Adds or modifies resources without deleting existing ones.
- **Complete**: Removes any resources not defined in the template.

Specify mode in CLI:

```
az deployment group create \
—mode Complete \
—resource-group myrg \
—template-file azuredeploy.json
```

Be cautious: Complete mode can delete unintended resources.

Best Practices

- **Use parameters** to make templates flexible and reusable.
- **Validate templates** before deploying:

AZ DEPLOYMENT GROUP validate \

—resource-group myrg \

—template-file azuredeploy.json

- **Use template specs** to centrally manage production-ready templates.
- **Version your templates** with Git for traceability.
- **Break large templates** into smaller linked templates.
- **Use dependsOn** to control deployment order explicitly.
- **Secure secrets** with Key Vault references instead of inline values.

Example of secure parameter:

"adminPassword": {

"reference": {

"keyVault": {

```
"id": "/subscriptions/xxx/resourceGroups/rg/providers/Microsoft.KeyVault/vaults/mykv"
},
"secretName": "vmPassword"
}
}
```

Troubleshooting Deployments

COMMON ISSUES INCLUDE:

- **Schema mismatch**: Ensure $schema URL matches resource types and API versions.
- **Missing dependencies**: Use dependsOn where needed.
- **Invalid parameter values**: Use allowedValues to restrict.
- **Incorrect resource names**: Validate DNS or naming rules.
- **Quota limits exceeded**: Check subscription limits for compute, network, etc.

Use deployment logs for troubleshooting:

```
az deployment group show \
—name mydeployment \
—resource-group myrg
```

ARM vs Bicep

BICEP IS A DOMAIN-SPECIFIC language (DSL) that simplifies ARM syntax. It is transpiled into ARM JSON templates and is considered the future of Azure IaC.

Feature	ARM (JSON)	Bicep
Syntax	Verbose, strict JSON	Concise, declarative language
Tooling	CLI, Portal, Visual Studio	CLI, VS Code Extension
Readability	Moderate	High
Compilation	Native	Requires transpilation

Example: Bicep version of storage account

```
resource stg 'Microsoft.Storage/storageAccounts@2022-09-01' = {

name: 'mystorageacct'

location: 'uksouth'

sku: {

name: 'Standard_LRS'

}

kind: 'StorageV2'

}
```

Summary

ARM TEMPLATES ARE A powerful mechanism for automating the provisioning and configuration of Azure infrastructure. By using declarative JSON syntax, parameters, and deployment orchestration,

Azure Administrators can build repeatable, version-controlled, and auditable infrastructure pipelines. Whether used independently or in conjunction with Bicep, CI/CD tools, or deployment scripts, mastering ARM templates is a critical skill for managing modern Azure environments at scale.

Configuring High Availability and Scalability

IN CLOUD ENVIRONMENTS, applications and workloads must remain resilient and performant regardless of failures, maintenance events, or spikes in usage. Azure offers a variety of features to ensure high availability (HA) and scalability (horizontal and vertical) for virtual machines and services. As an Azure Administrator, it's essential to understand and implement these features to deliver reliable and efficient solutions.

This section explores the core concepts, architecture patterns, and practical implementations of high availability and scalability in the context of Azure compute resources—especially Virtual Machines (VMs)—with a focus on ensuring uptime, handling failovers, distributing load, and autoscaling in response to real-time demand.

High Availability: Ensuring Uptime

HIGH AVAILABILITY IN Azure means designing systems to minimize downtime during planned or unplanned events. Azure provides both **intra-region** and **cross-region** high availability strategies.

Availability Sets

AN AVAILABILITY SET is a logical grouping that ensures VM workloads are spread across multiple physical resources within a single datacenter.

- **Fault Domains (FDs)**: Represent physical server racks. VMs in different FDs don't share power or network.
- **Update Domains (UDs)**: Ensure VMs are rebooted at different times during updates.

Deploying VMs in an availability set ensures at least one VM remains operational during maintenance or hardware failures.

```
az vm availability-set create \
—name myAvailSet \
—resource-group myRG \
—platform-fault-domain-count 2 \
—platform-update-domain-count 5 \
—location uksouth
```

Assign VMs to the availability set during creation:

```
az vm create \
—name myVM1 \
—resource-group myRG \
—availability-set myAvailSet \
—image UbuntuLTS \
```

—admin-username azureuser \

—generate-ssh-keys

Availability Zones

AVAILABILITY ZONES are physically separate datacenters within an Azure region. VMs deployed in different zones remain resilient to datacenter-level outages.

- Each region supports up to three zones.
- Zonal VMs provide SLAs up to 99.99% uptime.

Create a VM in a specific zone:

az vm create \

—resource-group myRG \

—name zonedVM \

—image UbuntuLTS \

—zone 2 \

—admin-username azureuser \

—generate-ssh-keys

For higher abstraction, use **Zone Redundant Services** (e.g., Azure SQL, Load Balancer) that automatically span zones.

Proximity Placement Groups

USED TO CO-LOCATE VMS as close as possible to minimize latency. Useful for tightly coupled workloads like high-performance databases.

az ppg create \

—name myPPG \

—resource-group myRG \

—location uksouth \

—intent lowLatency

Attach VMs to the PPG during creation.

Scalability: Meeting Demand

SCALABILITY IN AZURE refers to the ability to adjust resources based on workload requirements. This includes:

- **Vertical scaling**: Changing VM size (CPU/RAM).
- **Horizontal scaling**: Adding/removing instances.

Azure supports both manual and automatic scaling mechanisms.

Virtual Machine Scale Sets (VMSS)

VMSS ALLOW YOU TO DEPLOY and manage a group of identical, load-balanced VMs. They support autoscaling and integrate with load balancers, availability zones, and monitoring tools.

Key Features:

- Uniform configuration across instances
- Auto-repair and health monitoring
- Custom or platform images
- Integration with Azure Load Balancer and Application Gateway

CREATE A SCALE SET with autoscaling:

az vmss create \

—resource-group myRG \

—name myScaleSet \

—image UbuntuLTS \

—upgrade-policy-mode automatic \

—custom-data cloud-init.txt \

—admin-username azureuser \

—generate-ssh-keys \

—vm-sku Standard_D2s_v3 \

—instance-count 2 \

—load-balancer myLB

Enable autoscaling rules:

az monitor autoscale create \

—resource-group myRG \

—resource myScaleSet \

—resource-type Microsoft.Compute/virtualMachineScaleSets \

—name autoscaleRule \

—min-count 2 \

—max-count 5 \

—count 2

Add a CPU-based scaling rule:

az monitor autoscale rule create \

—resource-group myRG \

—autoscale-name autoscaleRule \

—condition "Percentage CPU > 75 avg 5m" \

—scale out 1

Load Balancing for Scalability

AZURE PROVIDES SEVERAL load balancing options:

Azure Load Balancer (Layer 4)

- Distributes TCP/UDP traffic across VMs
- Supports inbound and outbound NAT
- Ideal for VMSS, VMs in availability sets

EXAMPLE:

az network lb create \

—resource-group myRG \

—name myLoadBalancer \

—sku Standard \

—frontend-ip-name myFrontend \

—backend-pool-name myBackendPool

Attach VMs to backend pool:

az network nic ip-config address-pool add \

—address-pool myBackendPool \

—ip-config-name ipconfig1 \

—nic-name myVMNIC \

—resource-group myRG \

—lb-name myLoadBalancer

Azure Application Gateway (Layer 7)

- HTTP/S load balancing
- SSL termination and WAF integration
- URL-based routing, session affinity

BEST FOR WEB APPLICATIONS and APIs.

Azure Autoscale and Monitoring

USE **Azure Monitor** with autoscale settings to scale out/in based on metrics like:

- CPU utilization
- Memory usage (via custom metrics)
- Queue length
- Custom application metrics (via Log Analytics or Application Insights)

Monitor VMSS instance health and trigger actions using **Action Groups**:

```
az monitor action-group create \
—name vmScaleAlertGroup \
—resource-group myRG \
—short-name vmAlert \
—email-admins true \
—email-receivers name=admin email=admin@example.com
```

High Availability for State-Dependent Workloads

FOR WORKLOADS LIKE databases:

- Use Azure SQL Database with geo-replication and auto-failover.

- Use PostgreSQL Flexible Server in zone-redundant configuration.
- For IaaS DBs (e.g., SQL Server), configure Always On availability groups.
- Use **shared disks** with Azure VMs for cluster configurations (e.g., SAP, WSFC).

Maintenance and Reliability Strategies

- Enable **automatic OS image upgrades** for VMSS.
- Use **automatic instance repair** for VMSS to maintain health.
- Implement **Azure Backup** and **Azure Site Recovery** for DR.
- Apply **update domains** in availability sets for patching resilience.
- Perform **rolling updates** using custom scripts or DevOps pipelines.

Best Practices

- Use **Availability Zones** whenever possible.
- Choose **VMSS** over manually managed VM clusters.
- Use **Load Balancer** for stateless workloads; **App Gateway** for HTTP/S.

- Implement **autoscaling** to reduce costs and handle peaks.
- Monitor aggressively with **Azure Monitor**, **Log Analytics**, and **Application Insights**.
- Apply **naming conventions and tagging** for grouped resources.
- Regularly test **failover scenarios** and document recovery procedures.

Summary

HIGH AVAILABILITY AND scalability are not optional in production-grade cloud environments—they are essential. Azure offers a rich set of tools and services, including availability sets, availability zones, scale sets, load balancers, and autoscaling mechanisms, that allow organizations to design resilient, responsive, and cost-effective infrastructure. By combining these features effectively, Azure Administrators can ensure business continuity, meet SLAs, and support dynamic application workloads without manual intervention.

Managing VM Backups and Monitoring

EFFECTIVE MANAGEMENT of virtual machines in Azure extends beyond deployment and configuration—it includes protecting workloads from data loss and monitoring their health and performance continuously. Azure provides robust services like Azure Backup and Azure Monitor to support business continuity, ensure compliance, reduce operational risks, and maintain the performance of virtualized environments.

This section covers how to configure and manage backups for Azure VMs, monitor resource utilization, set up alerts, and integrate with Log Analytics for deeper observability and operational intelligence.

Azure VM Backup Overview

AZURE BACKUP IS A CENTRALIZED, scalable, and secure solution for backing up and restoring Azure virtual machines. It's built into the Azure platform and integrates directly with Recovery Services Vaults.

Key Features:

- Application-consistent snapshots
- Long-term retention
- Daily, weekly, monthly, and yearly backup policies
- Point-in-time recovery
- Built-in monitoring and alerting

Backups use the **VMSnapshot** extension, ensuring crash and file-system consistency. For certain workloads, such as SQL Server or SAP HANA on Azure VMs, workload-aware backup agents are also available.

Setting Up Azure Backup

Step 1: Create a Recovery Services Vault

AZ BACKUP VAULT CREATE \

—name myRecoveryVault \

—resource-group myRG \

—location uksouth

Step 2: Register the VM with the Vault

AZ BACKUP PROTECTABLE-item list \

—vault-name myRecoveryVault \

—resource-group myRG \

—workload-type AzureVM

Enable protection:

az backup protection enable-for-vm \

—vault-name myRecoveryVault \

—resource-group myRG \

—vm myVM \

—policy-name DefaultPolicy

Configuring Backup Policies

AZURE BACKUP POLICIES define the **frequency** and **retention** of restore points.

Example: Create a custom policy that backs up daily at 2:00 AM and retains backups for 30 days.

az backup policy create \

—name dailyPolicy \

```
—resource-group myRG \
—vault-name myRecoveryVault \
—policy "$(cat backupPolicy.json)"
```

Sample backupPolicy.json:

```
{
"properties": {
"schedulePolicy": {
"schedulePolicyType": "SimpleSchedulePolicy",
"scheduleRunFrequency": "Daily",
"scheduleRunTimes": ["2024-12-01T02:00:00Z"]
},
"retentionPolicy": {
"retentionPolicyType": "SimpleRetentionPolicy",
"dailySchedule": {
"retentionTimes": ["2024-12-01T02:00:00Z"],
"retentionDuration": {
"count": 30,
"durationType": "Days"
}
}
```

```
},
"backupManagementType": "AzureIaasVM"
}
}
```

Restoring a VM

AZURE BACKUP ALLOWS you to:

- Restore the full VM
- Restore individual disks
- Restore to original or alternate resource group

Restore full VM:

```
az backup recoverypoint list \
—vault-name myRecoveryVault \
—resource-group myRG \
—container-name myVM \
—item-name myVM
az backup restore restore-disks \
—vault-name myRecoveryVault \
—resource-group myRG \
—container-name myVM \
—item-name myVM \
```

—recovery-point-id <recoveryPointId> \

—storage-account mystorageacct

You can also restore directly from the Azure Portal by browsing to the vault → backup items → VM → Restore.

Backup Security and Compliance

- Backups are encrypted using Azure Storage Service Encryption (SSE).
- Soft-delete protects backups for 14 additional days after deletion.
- Azure RBAC controls access to backup configuration and restore operations.
- Long-term retention supports compliance (HIPAA, GDPR, ISO 27001).

ENABLE SOFT DELETE:

az backup vault backup-properties set \

—vault-name myRecoveryVault \

—resource-group myRG \

—soft-delete-feature-state Enabled

Azure Monitor Overview

AZURE MONITOR PROVIDES end-to-end observability into applications, infrastructure, and networks. For Azure VMs, it includes:

- **Metrics**: Performance data (CPU, disk, memory)
- **Logs**: Operational and diagnostic information
- **Alerts**: Rule-based triggers for thresholds or anomalies
- **Insights**: Preconfigured visualizations for VMs

Enabling Monitoring for VMs

Enable Diagnostic Settings

AZ MONITOR DIAGNOSTIC-settings create \

—name VMInsightsDiag \

—resource "/subscriptions/xxx/resourceGroups/myRG/providers/Microsoft.Compute/virtualMachines/myVM" \

—workspace "/subscriptions/xxx/resourceGroups/logsRG/providers/Microsoft.OperationalInsights/workspaces/myLogWorkspace" \

—logs '[{"category": "AllMetrics", "enabled": true}]'

Enable VM Insights

VM INSIGHTS PROVIDES pre-built dashboards and analytics.

az monitor vm insights enable \

—resource-group myRG \

—vm-name myVM \

—workspace myLogWorkspace

Analyzing Metrics

USE THE AZURE PORTAL or CLI to review performance metrics:

az monitor metrics list \

—resource "/subscriptions/xxx/resourceGroups/myRG/providers/Microsoft.Compute/virtualMachines/myVM" \

—metric "Percentage CPU"

Metrics include:

- CPU utilization
- Disk I/O
- Network throughput
- Guest OS metrics (via Log Analytics)

Querying Logs with Kusto (KQL)

EXAMPLE: IDENTIFY CPU usage spikes across all VMs

Perf

| where ObjectName == "Processor" and CounterName == "% Processor Time"

| summarize avg(CounterValue) by Computer, bin(TimeGenerated, 5m)

| order by avg_CounterValue desc

Example: List top 5 VMs by disk read latency

Perf

| where ObjectName == "LogicalDisk" and CounterName == "Avg. Disk sec/Read"

| summarize avg(CounterValue) by Computer

| top 5 by avg_CounterValue desc

Setting Alerts

CONFIGURE ALERTS FOR critical thresholds or operational anomalies.

Example: Alert for high CPU usage:

az monitor metrics alert create \

—name HighCPUAlert \

—resource-group myRG \

—scopes "/subscriptions/xxx/resourceGroups/myRG/providers/Microsoft.Compute/virtualMachines/myVM" \

—condition "avg Percentage CPU > 80" \

—description "CPU usage over 80%" \

—window-size 5m \

—evaluation-frequency 1m \

—action-group myAlertGroup

Action Groups

ACTION GROUPS DEFINE notification or remediation actions:

- Email, SMS, Webhook
- Logic Apps
- Azure Functions
- ITSM Integration

```
az monitor action-group create \
—name myAlertGroup \
—resource-group myRG \
—short-name alertGrp \
—email-receivers name=admin email=admin@example.com
```

Integration with Automation

AZURE MONITOR AND BACKUP can trigger automation tasks such as:

- VM restart upon failed heartbeat
- Autoscaling based on custom metrics
- Notification of backup failures
- Ticket creation in ITSM systems

Use Logic Apps or Azure Automation runbooks for end-to-end remediation.

Best Practices

- Use **Recovery Services Vault** with clearly defined policies.
- Enable **VM Backup** immediately after VM deployment.
- Test restore processes **regularly**.
- Monitor **backup health reports** and set failure alerts.
- Use **Log Analytics** for granular monitoring and troubleshooting.
- Combine **metrics and logs** for full-stack visibility.
- Secure vaults and diagnostic settings using **RBAC** and **managed identities**.
- Integrate monitoring into **CI/CD pipelines** for automated infrastructure compliance.

Summary

MANAGING VIRTUAL MACHINE backups and monitoring in Azure ensures data durability, business continuity, and operational visibility. Azure Backup enables secure and automated protection of VM workloads, while Azure Monitor provides deep insights into performance and behavior. By combining these tools with proper automation and alerting, Azure Administrators can proactively address issues, meet compliance requirements, and maintain optimal infrastructure health across dynamic environments.

Azure App Services and Container Instances

MODERN APPLICATIONS demand a deployment environment that is scalable, resilient, and easy to manage. Azure App Services and Azure Container Instances (ACI) provide two distinct but complementary solutions for running applications in the cloud without managing the underlying infrastructure. Both services align with Platform-as-a-Service (PaaS) principles and enable developers and administrators to focus on code and configuration rather than virtual machines, operating systems, or patching.

This section explores how to provision, configure, deploy, scale, and monitor applications using Azure App Services and Azure Container Instances, while also comparing their capabilities and ideal use cases for Azure Administrators.

Azure App Services Overview

AZURE APP SERVICE IS a fully managed PaaS platform for hosting web apps, REST APIs, and mobile backends. It supports .NET, Java, PHP, Node.js, Python, and custom containers.

Core Features

- Automatic scaling and high availability
- Built-in CI/CD integration
- Custom domain and SSL support
- Authentication and authorization
- VNet integration

- Deployment slots
- Diagnostic and logging features

APP SERVICES IS OPTIMIZED for **stateful, long-running** applications, particularly web-based workloads.

Creating an Azure App Service

TO DEPLOY AN APPLICATION, you must first create an **App Service Plan** and a **Web App**.

Step 1: Create an App Service Plan

AZ APPSERVICE PLAN create \

—name myAppServicePlan \

—resource-group myRG \

—sku S1 \

—is-linux \

—location uksouth

S1 indicates a Standard tier plan (includes auto-scaling and custom domains).

Step 2: Create the Web App

AZ WEBAPP CREATE \

—name myWebApp123 \

—resource-group myRG \

—plan myAppServicePlan \

—runtime "NODE|18-lts" \

—deployment-local-git

This returns a Git URL you can use to push your app source.

Deployment Options

YOU CAN DEPLOY CODE to Azure App Services using:

- **GitHub Actions / Azure DevOps Pipelines**
- **FTP or FTPS**
- **Local Git repositories**
- **Azure CLI or PowerShell**
- **Zip deploy**
- **Docker container registry (ACR or Docker Hub)**

Example: Deploy a zip package

az webapp deployment source config-zip \

—resource-group myRG \

—name myWebApp123 \

—src app.zip

To deploy from Docker Hub:

az webapp create \

—resource-group myRG \

—plan myAppServicePlan \

—name myDockerWebApp \

—deployment-container-image-name nginx

Scaling App Services

APP SERVICES SUPPORTS **manual** and **automatic scaling** based on:

- CPU utilization
- Memory usage
- HTTP request count
- Custom metrics via Azure Monitor

Enable autoscaling:

az monitor autoscale create \

—resource-group myRG \

—resource myAppServicePlan \

—resource-type Microsoft.Web/serverfarms \

—name autoscaleApp \

—min-count 1 \

—max-count 5 \

—count 2

Add a rule based on CPU:

```
az monitor autoscale rule create \
—resource-group myRG \
—autoscale-name autoscaleApp \
—condition "Percentage CPU > 70 avg 5m" \
—scale out 1
```

Deployment Slots

SLOTS ALLOW DEPLOYING new versions alongside the production version. You can **swap slots** with zero downtime.

Create a slot:

```
az webapp deployment slot create \
—name myWebApp123 \
—resource-group myRG \
—slot staging
```

Swap to production:

```
az webapp deployment slot swap \
—name myWebApp123 \
—resource-group myRG \
—slot staging
```

Monitoring and Diagnostics

ENABLE DIAGNOSTICS logs:

az webapp log config \

—name myWebApp123 \

—resource-group myRG \

—application-logging true \

—level information

Stream logs:

az webapp log tail \

—name myWebApp123 \

—resource-group myRG

Logs can also be sent to:

- Azure Monitor
- Log Analytics
- Storage Account

Use App Insights for deep diagnostics and telemetry.

Azure Container Instances (ACI) Overview

AZURE CONTAINER INSTANCES is a lightweight, serverless container service that allows you to run Docker containers without managing VMs or orchestrators like Kubernetes.

Key Features

- Fast startup (<1 minute)
- Supports Linux and Windows containers
- Pay-per-second billing
- Public or VNet-based deployments
- Multi-container support using YAML
- Ideal for short-lived or burst workloads

ACI IS OPTIMIZED FOR **stateless, event-driven** compute scenarios.

Creating a Container Instance

DEPLOY A CONTAINER using the Azure CLI:

```
az container create \
—name myContainer \
—resource-group myRG \
—image mcr.microsoft.com/azuredocs/aci-helloworld \
—cpu 1—memory 1 \
—dns-name-label mycontainerdns \
—ports 80
```

Output includes the FQDN to access your container.

To deploy a container from Azure Container Registry (ACR):

```
az container create \
—resource-group myRG \
—name myPrivateContainer \
—image myregistry.azurecr.io/myimage:latest \
—registry-login-server myregistry.azurecr.io \
—registry-username <username> \
—registry-password <password>
```

Networking Options

ACI SUPPORTS:

- Public IP address (default)
- Private IP via **VNet integration**

To deploy into a VNet:

```
az container create \
—resource-group myRG \
—name myVnetContainer \
—image myimage \
—vnet myVnet \
—subnet mySubnet \
—cpu 2 \
```

—memory 2

This allows containers to securely interact with backend resources.

Volumes and Persistent Storage

ACI CAN MOUNT:

- Azure File Shares
- Secrets
- EmptyDir

Example using Azure Files:

az container create \

—resource-group myRG \

—name myContainer \

—image nginx \

—azure-file-volume-share-name myfileshare \

—azure-file-volume-account-name mystorageacct \

—azure-file-volume-account-key <key> \

—azure-file-volume-mount-path /mnt/files

Monitoring Containers

GET LOGS:

az container logs \

—resource-group myRG \

—name myContainer

View container status:

az container show \

—resource-group myRG \

—name myContainer \

—query "{Status: instanceView.state, Events: instanceView.events}"

ACI logs can also be shipped to Azure Monitor or Event Hub.

App Service vs. Container Instances

Feature	Azure App Service	Azure Container Instances
Ideal Use Case	Web apps, APIs, backends	Short-lived tasks, batch jobs
Scaling	Auto and manual	Manual (or scripted with Logic Apps)
Deployment Time	Minutes	Seconds
VNet Integration	Yes (Premium plans)	Yes
Custom Domains & SSL	Yes	No native support
CI/CD Support	Deeply integrated	Requires scripting
Statefulness	Stateful	Stateless
Persistent Storage	Limited (App Settings, Files)	Azure Files, secrets, etc.

Best Practices

- Use **App Services** for continuously running production web apps.
- Use **Container Instances** for burst compute, pipelines, or cron-like workloads.
- Secure access using **managed identities** and **VNet integration**.
- Deploy App Services using **slots** for safe rollouts.
- Keep images lightweight for fast startup in ACI.
- Use **Azure Container Registry (ACR)** for image storage and lifecycle control.
- Apply **tags** and **naming standards** to keep deployments manageable.
- Monitor continuously with **App Insights** or **Log Analytics**.

Summary

AZURE APP SERVICES and Azure Container Instances simplify the deployment and management of modern applications. App Services provide a powerful, managed platform for web apps and APIs, while Container Instances offer lightweight, ephemeral execution environments for containerized workloads. By selecting the right service based on workload characteristics—stateful vs stateless, long-running vs short-lived—Azure Administrators can optimize both cost and performance, delivering cloud-native solutions with minimal operational overhead.

Chapter 5: Configuring and Managing Virtual Networks

Fundamentals of Azure Networking

IN AZURE, THE FOUNDATION of all compute, database, and storage resources begins with networking. Understanding Azure Virtual Networks (VNets) is essential for administrators responsible for deploying secure, scalable, and highly available infrastructure. VNets enable secure communication between resources, the internet, and on-premises environments, forming the backbone of connectivity in the Azure ecosystem.

This section provides a comprehensive introduction to the key concepts, architecture, and configuration steps associated with Azure networking. It emphasizes the structure and function of VNets, subnets, IP addressing, DNS, service endpoints, and more.

Virtual Network (VNet) Basics

AN AZURE VIRTUAL NETWORK is a **logical isolation of the Azure cloud** dedicated to your subscription. It is analogous to a traditional network in a data center, with additional benefits such as scalability, availability, and isolation.

Key Properties:

- IPv4 (and optional IPv6) address space
- One or more subnets
- Custom DNS support

- Route tables and network security groups
- Peering for connectivity across VNets
- Integration with VPN and ExpressRoute

A VNET SPANS A SINGLE region, but peering can enable cross-region connectivity.

Creating a Virtual Network

Using the Azure Portal:

1. Go to **Create a resource > Networking > Virtual Network**
2. Define:

○ Name: myVNet

○ Region: UK South

○ Address space: 10.0.0.0/16

○ Subnet: 10.0.1.0/24

Using Azure CLI:

AZ NETWORK VNET CREATE \

—resource-group myRG \

—name myVNet \

—address-prefix 10.0.0.0/16 \

—subnet-name default \

—subnet-prefix 10.0.1.0/24

You can create additional subnets later using:

az network vnet subnet create \

—resource-group myRG \

—vnet-name myVNet \

—name appSubnet \

—address-prefix 10.0.2.0/24

Subnets

SUBNETS DIVIDE A VNET'S IP address space into smaller segments to allocate resources logically and enforce security boundaries.

Best Practices:

- Use subnet naming conventions (e.g., webSubnet, dbSubnet)
- Assign specific address ranges for each role/ environment
- Isolate workloads (e.g., app vs DB) into separate subnets

Example structure:

- VNet: 10.0.0.0/16
  - Subnet 1: 10.0.1.0/24 (Web)

  - Subnet 2: 10.0.2.0/24 (App)
  - Subnet 3: 10.0.3.0/24 (Database)

IP Addressing

VNETS AND SUBNETS MUST be assigned private IPv4 ranges using RFC 1918:

- 10.0.0.0 – 10.255.255.255
- 172.16.0.0 – 172.31.255.255
- 192.168.0.0 – 192.168.255.255

Azure assigns dynamic private IPs to VMs by default but supports static private IPs if required:

az network nic ip-config update \

—resource-group myRG \

—nic-name myNIC \

—name ipconfig1 \

—private-ip-address 10.0.1.10

Public IPs are created separately and can be assigned to VMs or load balancers.

az network public-ip create \

—resource-group myRG \

—name myPublicIP \

—allocation-method Static

DNS in VNets

BY DEFAULT, VNETS USE Azure-provided DNS (168.63.129.16). You can override this with custom DNS servers.

az network vnet update \

—name myVNet \

—resource-group myRG \

—dns-servers 10.0.0.4 10.0.0.5

Use cases for custom DNS:

- Integrate with on-prem Active Directory DNS
- Use third-party DNS for advanced filtering
- Host internal zones for private domains

Network Security Groups (NSGs)

NSGS ALLOW OR DENY traffic to VMs, subnets, and other Azure resources. Rules are based on:

- Source/Destination IP or tag (e.g., Internet, VirtualNetwork)
- Protocol (TCP/UDP)
- Port ranges
- Priority (lower number = higher priority)

- Action (Allow/Deny)

Example: Allow SSH to VMs

az network nsg rule create \

—resource-group myRG \

—nsg-name myNSG \

—name AllowSSH \

—priority 100 \

—direction Inbound \

—access Allow \

—protocol Tcp \

—destination-port-range 22 \

—source-address-prefix Internet

Apply NSG to subnet:

az network vnet subnet update \

—resource-group myRG \

—vnet-name myVNet \

—name appSubnet \

—network-security-group myNSG

Service Endpoints

SERVICE ENDPOINTS EXTEND your VNet's private address space to Azure services, such as:

- Azure Storage
- Azure SQL Database
- Azure Key Vault

They provide secure, optimized routing and eliminate the need for public IPs.

Enable a service endpoint:

az network vnet subnet update \

—name appSubnet \

—vnet-name myVNet \

—resource-group myRG \

—service-endpoints Microsoft.Storage

Private Endpoints

PRIVATE ENDPOINTS ALLOW Azure services (like Storage or SQL) to appear on your VNet with a private IP.

Use cases:

- Replace service endpoints for enhanced security
- Avoid public exposure completely

- Simplify NSG and firewall rules

Create a private endpoint:

az network private-endpoint create \

—name myPrivateEndpoint \

—resource-group myRG \

—vnet-name myVNet \

—subnet appSubnet \

—private-connection-resource-id "/subscriptions/.../Microsoft.Storage/storageAccounts/mystorageacct" \

—group-id blob \

—connection-name myPrivateConnection

Routing and UDRs

AZURE AUTOMATICALLY creates system routes, but you can override them using **User Defined Routes (UDRs)** for:

- Force tunneling to NVA (network virtual appliance)
- Custom next-hop configuration
- Isolating traffic flows

Create a route table and route:

az network route-table create \

—name myRouteTable \

—resource-group myRG

az network route-table route create \

—resource-group myRG \

—route-table-name myRouteTable \

—name routeToFirewall \

—address-prefix 0.0.0.0/0 \

—next-hop-type VirtualAppliance \

—next-hop-ip-address 10.0.1.4

Associate with subnet:

az network vnet subnet update \

—vnet-name myVNet \

—name appSubnet \

—resource-group myRG \

—route-table myRouteTable

VNet Peering

VNET PEERING CONNECTS two VNets within the same or different regions, enabling private IP communication across them.

Use Cases:

- Multi-region architecture
- Shared services model

- Dev-test separation

CREATE A PEERING:

az network vnet peering create \

—name peerToProd \

—resource-group myRG \

—vnet-name devVNet \

—remote-vnet /subscriptions/.../resourceGroups/prodRG/providers/Microsoft.Network/virtualNetworks/prodVNet \

—allow-vnet-access

Peering is non-transitive—if A peers with B, and B with C, A does **not** automatically talk to C.

Best Practices

- Use CIDR blocks with room for future subnet expansion.

- Reserve IP ranges for peering and hybrid networking.

- Use NSGs at the subnet level for easier management.

- Disable default routes with 0.0.0.0/0 only if using custom firewalls or NVAs.

- Use Private Endpoints over service endpoints for higher security.

- Apply tagging (env, role, team) for all VNets and subnets.

- Monitor with Network Watcher for packet capture and topology.

Summary

VIRTUAL NETWORKS FORM the core of Azure infrastructure design. A well-architected VNet ensures secure, performant, and scalable interconnectivity for cloud-based workloads. By mastering subnets, IP address management, security groups, service/private endpoints, and peering, Azure Administrators can create robust network architectures that support modern cloud-native and hybrid deployments. Understanding these fundamentals is a prerequisite to implementing advanced features such as VPN gateways, Azure Firewall, and custom routing.

Configuring Virtual Networks and Subnets

CREATING AND MANAGING Azure Virtual Networks (VNets) and subnets is foundational to deploying secure, scalable, and segmented network topologies. VNets allow Azure resources like virtual machines, databases, and web apps to securely communicate with each other, the internet, and on-premises networks. Subnets further segment VNets to apply security boundaries, enforce routing rules, and organize workloads for administrative clarity and scalability.

In this section, we will cover how to configure VNets and subnets using the Azure Portal, Azure CLI, and ARM templates. We will also explore best practices for IP address planning, DNS setup, service integrations, and subnet delegation for advanced services.

VNet and Subnet Planning

BEFORE CREATING A VNET, consider:

- **IP Address Space**: Define an IP range using RFC 1918 blocks.
- **Subnetting Strategy**: Break IP ranges into logical segments by function or workload (e.g., web, app, db).
- **Growth and Peering**: Plan address space with room for future services and VNet peering.
- **Security Zones**: Use subnets to enforce policy separation for security and compliance.

Example CIDR Design:

Subnet Name	CIDR Range	Purpose
WebSubnet	10.0.1.0/24	Front-end services
AppSubnet	10.0.2.0/24	Business logic
DBSubnet	10.0.3.0/24	Database workloads
BastionSubnet	10.0.4.0/27	Azure Bastion

Creating a Virtual Network

Azure CLI

AZ NETWORK VNET CREATE \

—name MyVNet \

—resource-group MyResourceGroup \

—address-prefix 10.1.0.0/16 \

—location uksouth \

—subnet-name WebSubnet \

—subnet-prefix 10.1.1.0/24

This command creates both the VNet and a subnet.

To add additional subnets:

az network vnet subnet create \

—resource-group MyResourceGroup \

—vnet-name MyVNet \

—name AppSubnet \

—address-prefix 10.1.2.0/24

DNS Configuration for VNets

BY DEFAULT, VNETS USE Azure-provided DNS. You can override this setting for custom domain name resolution.

az network vnet update \

—name MyVNet \

—resource-group MyResourceGroup \

—dns-servers 10.0.0.4 10.0.0.5

This is often required for hybrid networks using on-premises Active Directory or custom internal DNS.

Subnet Delegation

DELEGATION ALLOWS SUBNETS to be assigned to specific Azure services, such as:

- Azure Kubernetes Service (AKS)
- Azure NetApp Files
- Azure App Service Environments

Example: Delegate subnet to Microsoft.Web/serverFarms:

az network vnet subnet update \

—resource-group MyResourceGroup \

—vnet-name MyVNet \

—name AppServiceSubnet \

—delegations Microsoft.Web/serverFarms

Once delegated, the subnet will enforce specific rules compatible with the service.

Subnet Network Security Groups (NSGs)

YOU CAN ASSIGN NSGS to a subnet to control traffic flow in and out. NSGs apply to all resources in the subnet.

az network nsg create \

—name WebNSG \

—resource-group MyResourceGroup

az network vnet subnet update \

—vnet-name MyVNet \

—name WebSubnet \

—resource-group MyResourceGroup \

—network-security-group WebNSG

Route Tables (User Defined Routes)

ROUTE TABLES CUSTOMIZE how traffic flows between subnets or through appliances like firewalls or NVAs.

az network route-table create \

—name AppRouteTable \

—resource-group MyResourceGroup

az network route-table route create \

—resource-group MyResourceGroup \

—route-table-name AppRouteTable \

—name RouteToFirewall \

—address-prefix 0.0.0.0/0 \

—next-hop-type VirtualAppliance \

—next-hop-ip-address 10.0.0.4

Apply the route table to a subnet:

az network vnet subnet update \

—vnet-name MyVNet \

—name AppSubnet \

—resource-group MyResourceGroup \

—route-table AppRouteTable

Integrating Azure Services

MANY SERVICES, SUCH as Azure App Service, Azure SQL, and Storage Accounts, can be integrated with VNets through:

- **Service Endpoints**: Extend VNet identity to PaaS services.
- **Private Endpoints**: Assign a private IP to the service within the subnet.

Adding Service Endpoint

AZ NETWORK VNET SUBNET update \

—name AppSubnet \

—vnet-name MyVNet \

—resource-group MyResourceGroup \

—service-endpoints Microsoft.Storage

Creating Private Endpoint

AZ NETWORK PRIVATE-endpoint create \

—name MyPrivateEndpoint \

—resource-group MyResourceGroup \

—vnet-name MyVNet \

—subnet AppSubnet \

—private-connection-resource-id /subscriptions/.../Microsoft.Storage/storageAccounts/myStorageAcct \

—group-id blob \

—connection-name MyPrivateConnection

Deploying VNets and Subnets via ARM Template

{

"$schema": "https://schema.management.azure.com/schemas/2019-04-01/deploymentTemplate.json#",

"contentVersion": "1.0.0.0",

"resources": [

{

"type": "Microsoft.Network/virtualNetworks",

"apiVersion": "2022-09-01",

"name": "MyVNet",

"location": "uksouth",

"properties": {

"addressSpace": {

"addressPrefixes": ["10.2.0.0/16"]

```
},
"subnets": [
{
"name": "WebSubnet",
"properties": {
"addressPrefix": "10.2.1.0/24"
}
},
{
"name": "AppSubnet",
"properties": {
"addressPrefix": "10.2.2.0/24"
}
}
]
}
}
]
}
```

Deploy via Azure CLI:

```
az deployment group create \
—resource-group MyResourceGroup \
—template-file vnet-subnets.json
```

Monitoring and Troubleshooting

USE **Network Watcher** for:

- Topology mapping
- IP flow verify
- Connection troubleshoot
- Packet capture
- Next-hop analysis

Enable Network Watcher:

```
az network watcher configure \
—locations uksouth \
—resource-group MyResourceGroup \
—enabled true
```

Example: Trace route from VM to destination

```
az network watcher show-topology \
—resource-group MyResourceGroup \
—location uksouth
```

Best Practices

- Always leave buffer space in CIDR ranges for growth.
- Apply NSGs and route tables at the **subnet** level when possible.
- Delegate subnets to specific services for greater control.
- Use **naming conventions** like prod-vnet-core, sub-web-01, sub-db-01.
- Document VNet peering relationships and avoid IP overlaps.
- Group related subnets by **function** (e.g., web, app, db, management).
- Protect subnets with Azure Firewall, NSGs, and route filters.
- Use Private Endpoints to eliminate public exposure of services.

Summary

AZURE VIRTUAL NETWORKS and subnets form the structural foundation of secure and efficient cloud deployments. Proper configuration and segmentation of address spaces, along with controlled routing and access, allow Azure Administrators to build well-architected solutions that scale, remain resilient, and meet enterprise compliance requirements. Whether deploying for development environments or multi-region production workloads, careful planning and management of VNets and subnets is essential to Azure networking success.

Network Security Groups and Firewalls

SECURITY IS A FOUNDATIONAL element of cloud infrastructure. Azure offers a layered security model that enables administrators to control inbound and outbound traffic to and from resources in a Virtual Network. Two essential components in this model are **Network Security Groups (NSGs)** and **Azure Firewall.** These services work together to restrict unauthorized access, segment networks, and enforce compliance requirements.

In this section, we explore how to configure and manage NSGs and Azure Firewall, including best practices for securing subnets, virtual machines, and hybrid environments. We will also examine use cases, limitations, and how to integrate these tools into broader security architectures.

Network Security Groups (NSGs)

AN NSG IS A STATEFUL packet filtering firewall applied to **subnets** or **network interfaces** (NICs). It consists of inbound and outbound security rules that allow or deny traffic based on the following parameters:

- Source and destination IPs or service tags
- Source and destination ports
- Protocol (TCP/UDP/Any)
- Direction (Inbound/Outbound)

- Priority (100–4096; lower is higher priority)
- Access (Allow/Deny)

Default Rules

EVERY NSG INCLUDES three default rules:

1. **AllowVNetInBound** – Allows traffic between resources in the same VNet.
2. **AllowAzureLoadBalancerInBound** – Allows traffic from the Azure Load Balancer.
3. **DenyAllInbound/Outbound** – Denies all other traffic not explicitly allowed.

These default rules can't be deleted but can be overridden with higher priority custom rules.

Creating and Applying an NSG

Step 1: Create the NSG

AZ NETWORK NSG CREATE \

—name WebNSG \

—resource-group MyResourceGroup \

—location uksouth

Step 2: Add Rules

ALLOW HTTP TRAFFIC:

```
az network nsg rule create \
—resource-group MyResourceGroup \
—nsg-name WebNSG \
—name AllowHTTP \
—priority 100 \
—direction Inbound \
—access Allow \
—protocol Tcp \
—destination-port-range 80 \
—source-address-prefix Internet
```

Deny RDP from Internet:

```
az network nsg rule create \
—resource-group MyResourceGroup \
—nsg-name WebNSG \
—name DenyRDP \
—priority 200 \
—direction Inbound \
—access Deny \
—protocol Tcp \
—destination-port-range 3389 \
```

—source-address-prefix Internet

Step 3: Associate with Subnet or NIC

ASSOCIATE NSG WITH subnet:

az network vnet subnet update \

—vnet-name MyVNet \

—name WebSubnet \

—resource-group MyResourceGroup \

—network-security-group WebNSG

Associate NSG with a VM NIC:

az network nic update \

—name myVMNic \

—resource-group MyResourceGroup \

—network-security-group WebNSG

Service Tags and Application Security Groups

Service Tags

AZURE USES SERVICE tags to simplify rule creation for known services (e.g., Internet, VirtualNetwork, AzureLoadBalancer, Storage, Sql, etc.)

Example: Allow traffic from Azure Backup:

az network nsg rule create \

—resource-group MyResourceGroup \

—nsg-name WebNSG \

—name AllowBackup \

—priority 300 \

—direction Outbound \

—access Allow \

—protocol Tcp \

—destination-address-prefix AzureBackup \

—destination-port-range '*'

Application Security Groups (ASGs)

ASGS GROUP NICS LOGICALLY and apply NSG rules to these groups, reducing rule complexity in large deployments.

Create ASG:

az network asg create \

—resource-group MyResourceGroup \

—name WebServers

Apply ASG in NSG rule:

az network nsg rule create \

—resource-group MyResourceGroup \

—nsg-name WebNSG \

—name AllowAppToDB \

—priority 110 \

—direction Inbound \

—access Allow \

—protocol Tcp \

—source-asgs WebServers \

—destination-port-range 1433 \

—destination-address-prefixes 10.0.3.0/24

Azure Firewall

AZURE FIREWALL IS A managed, cloud-native, stateful firewall-as-a-service that offers high availability and unrestricted scalability. It provides centralized traffic control for VNets and hybrid connections and supports threat intelligence and logging.

Key Features:

- Inbound and outbound filtering
- Application and network rule support
- FQDN filtering
- Threat intelligence-based filtering
- TLS inspection (Premium tier)
- SNAT/DNAT

- Logging via Azure Monitor

Deploying Azure Firewall

Step 1: Create a Firewall Policy (optional)

AZ NETWORK FIREWALL policy create \

—name MyFirewallPolicy \

—resource-group MyResourceGroup \

—location uksouth

Step 2: Create Public IP

AZ NETWORK PUBLIC-IP create \

—name MyFirewallIP \

—resource-group MyResourceGroup \

—sku Standard \

—location uksouth \

—allocation-method Static

Step 3: Create Azure Firewall

AZ NETWORK FIREWALL create \

—name MyFirewall \

—resource-group MyResourceGroup \

—location uksouth \

—sku AZFW_VNet \

—vnet-name FirewallVNet \

—public-ip-address MyFirewallIP

Firewall Rules

Network Rules

PERMIT DNS (UDP 53):

az network firewall network-rule create \

—firewall-name MyFirewall \

—resource-group MyResourceGroup \

—collection-name DNSRules \

—name AllowDNS \

—rule-type NetworkRule \

—priority 100 \

—action Allow \

—rule-name AllowDNS \

—protocols UDP \

—source-addresses '*' \

—destination-addresses '*' \

—destination-ports 53

Application Rules

PERMIT ACCESS TO *.microsoft.com over HTTPS:

```
az network firewall application-rule create \
—firewall-name MyFirewall \
—resource-group MyResourceGroup \
—collection-name AppRules \
—name AllowMS \
—rule-type ApplicationRule \
—priority 200 \
—action Allow \
—rule-name AllowMicrosoft \
—protocols Http=80 Https=443 \
—target-fqdns "*.microsoft.com" \
—source-addresses 10.0.0.0/24
```

Integrating NSGs and Firewalls

BOTH NSGS AND AZURE Firewall can be used in a **hub-and-spoke** architecture:

- Use NSGs for **east-west** traffic filtering (within and between subnets).

- Use Azure Firewall for **north-south** traffic filtering (inbound/outbound to/from internet and on-premises).

Deploy Azure Firewall in the **hub VNet**, and connect spokes via VNet peering or Virtual WAN.

Route traffic to Azure Firewall via **User Defined Routes (UDRs)**:

az network route-table route create \

—resource-group MyResourceGroup \

—route-table-name MyRouteTable \

—name RouteToFirewall \

—address-prefix 0.0.0.0/0 \

—next-hop-type VirtualAppliance \

—next-hop-ip-address 10.0.0.4

Monitoring and Logging

USE **Azure Monitor** and **Diagnostic Settings** for:

- NSG Flow Logs
- Firewall traffic logs
- Alert rules for denied traffic

Enable flow logs:

az network watcher flow-log configure \

—nsg WebNSG \

—resource-group MyResourceGroup \

—enabled true \

—storage-account mystorageacct \

—retention 30

Firewall diagnostics:

az monitor diagnostic-settings create \

—resource "/subscriptions/.../resourceGroups/MyResourceGroup/providers/Microsoft.Network/azureFirewalls/MyFirewall" \

—name FWLogs \

—workspace "/subscriptions/.../resourceGroups/logsRG/providers/Microsoft.OperationalInsights/workspaces/myLogAnalytics" \

—logs '[{"category": "AzureFirewallNetworkRule", "enabled": true}]'

Best Practices

- Apply NSGs at the **subnet level** for broader control; override at NIC only if needed.
- Use **service tags** and **ASGs** to simplify NSG rule management.
- Deny all traffic by default, then explicitly allow what's needed.
- Deploy Azure Firewall in a **hub VNet** and centralize outbound filtering.

- Use **UDRs** to force outbound flows through the firewall.
- Monitor NSG and firewall logs with **Log Analytics** and set alerts.
- Use **just-in-time access** for admin ports like RDP/SSH.
- Segment critical resources into **isolated subnets** with tighter rules.
- Periodically audit rules using **Azure Policy** and **Security Center**.

Summary

NETWORK SECURITY GROUPS and Azure Firewall form a powerful combination for protecting resources in Azure. NSGs provide low-latency, granular traffic filtering at the subnet and NIC level, while Azure Firewall offers advanced, centralized, scalable protection for cloud and hybrid networks. Understanding how to configure, deploy, and integrate these tools is essential for any Azure Administrator responsible for ensuring network security, compliance, and operational integrity.

Implementing VNet Peering and VPNs

IN MODERN ENTERPRISE architectures, seamless and secure communication across distributed networks is critical. Azure provides multiple mechanisms for connecting virtual networks (VNets) and enabling hybrid connectivity with on-premises environments. Two key features in this realm are **VNet Peering**, which enables Azure-to-Azure connectivity, and **VPN Gateways**, which support secure encrypted tunnels between Azure and on-premises networks or other cloud providers.

This section explores the implementation of both VNet Peering and VPN connections in Azure, including their architecture, use cases, configuration steps, and best practices. Together, they form the foundation of connected, hybrid cloud networks.

VNet Peering Overview

VNET PEERING ALLOWS direct, low-latency connectivity between two virtual networks. Once peered, VNets can communicate with each other as if they were part of the same network, using private IPs.

Types of VNet Peering:

- **Intra-region Peering**: Between VNets in the same Azure region.
- **Global Peering**: Between VNets in different Azure regions.

Key Characteristics:

- No public internet traversal
- High bandwidth and low latency
- No downtime during setup
- Supports Resource Manager–only (not classic)

- Transitive peering is **not** supported

Creating VNet Peering

Scenario: Peer VNetA in uksouth with VNetB in westeurope

Step 1: Create VNets

AZ NETWORK VNET CREATE \

—name VNetA \

—resource-group RG1 \

—location uksouth \

—address-prefix 10.1.0.0/16 \

—subnet-name SubnetA

az network vnet create \

—name VNetB \

—resource-group RG2 \

—location westeurope \

—address-prefix 10.2.0.0/16 \

—subnet-name SubnetB

Step 2: Create Peering from VNetA to VNetB

AZ NETWORK VNET PEERING create \

—name PeerToB \

—resource-group RG1 \

—vnet-name VNetA \

—remote-vnet /subscriptions/<sub-id>/resourceGroups/RG2/providers/Microsoft.Network/virtualNetworks/VNetB \

—allow-vnet-access

Step 3: Create Peering from VNetB to VNetA

AZ NETWORK VNET PEERING create \

—name PeerToA \

—resource-group RG2 \

—vnet-name VNetB \

—remote-vnet /subscriptions/<sub-id>/resourceGroups/RG1/providers/Microsoft.Network/virtualNetworks/VNetA \

—allow-vnet-access

VNet Peering: Advanced Options

- **AllowForwardedTraffic**: Allows traffic forwarded by a VM in the remote VNet.
- **AllowGatewayTransit**: Lets one VNet use another's VPN gateway.
- **UseRemoteGateways**: Allows peered VNet to use the gateway in the hub VNet.

THESE ARE USEFUL IN hub-and-spoke topologies:

```
az network vnet peering update \
—resource-group RG2 \
—name PeerToA \
—vnet-name VNetB \
—set allowGatewayTransit=true
az network vnet peering update \
—resource-group RG1 \
—name PeerToB \
—vnet-name VNetA \
—set useRemoteGateways=true
```

VPN Gateway Overview

A VPN GATEWAY ENABLES encrypted traffic over public networks between:

- Azure VNets and on-premises networks (site-to-site)
- Azure VNets and other cloud providers (site-to-site)
- Azure VNets and individual devices (point-to-site)
- Multiple VNets (VNet-to-VNet)

VPN Gateways use industry-standard protocols like **IKEv2** and **IPsec**.

Types of Gateway Connections:

Type	Description
Site-to-Site	Connect on-premises to Azure VNet
Point-to-Site	Remote clients connect to Azure VNet
VNet-to-VNet	Connect multiple VNets securely
ExpressRoute	Dedicated circuit, not encrypted

Deploying a VPN Gateway

Step 1: Create Gateway Subnet

THE GATEWAY SUBNET must be named GatewaySubnet.

az network vnet subnet create \

—name GatewaySubnet \

—resource-group RG1 \

—vnet-name VNetA \

—address-prefix 10.1.255.0/27

Step 2: Create Public IP

AZ NETWORK PUBLIC-IP create \

—name VNetAGatewayIP \

—resource-group RG1 \

—allocation-method Dynamic

Step 3: Create VPN Gateway

AZ NETWORK VNET-GATEWAY create \

—name VNetAGateway \

—public-ip-address VNetAGatewayIP \

—resource-group RG1 \

—vnet VNetA \

—gateway-type Vpn \

—vpn-type RouteBased \

—sku VpnGw1 \

—no-wait

Site-to-Site VPN Configuration

On-Prem Setup Required:

- Public IP address (static)
- VPN device (Cisco, Fortinet, Juniper, etc.)
- Compatible configuration (can be generated in Azure)

Step 1: Create Local Network Gateway

AZ NETWORK LOCAL-GATEWAY create \

—name OnPremGateway \

```
—resource-group RG1 \
—gateway-ip-address <on-prem-IP> \
—local-address-prefixes 192.168.0.0/16
```

Step 2: Create the VPN Connection

```
AZ NETWORK VPN-CONNECTION create \
—name SiteToSiteConn \
—resource-group RG1 \
—vnet-gateway1 VNetAGateway \
—local-gateway2 OnPremGateway \
—shared-key SuperSecretKey123
```

VNet-to-VNet VPN

VPN CONNECTIONS CAN also link VNets across regions securely if peering is not an option.

Create both gateways, and then establish a connection between them.

```
az network vpn-connection create \
—name VNetToVNetConn \
—resource-group RG1 \
—vnet-gateway1 VNetAGateway \
—vnet-gateway2 VNetBGateway \
```

—shared-key VNetSecretKey

Point-to-Site VPN

THIS CONFIGURATION allows developers or administrators to connect their individual devices securely to a VNet.

Requirements:

- VPN Gateway with a route-based SKU
- Root and client certificates
- VPN client configuration (can be downloaded)

ENABLE POINT-TO-SITE:

az network vnet-gateway vpn-client generate \

—resource-group RG1 \

—name VNetAGateway

The output includes a VPN package to distribute to users.

Monitoring and Troubleshooting

USE **Network Watcher** to:

- Verify effective routes
- Check IP flow
- Monitor VPN Gateway connection status

Example: View VPN connection status

az network vpn-connection show \

—name SiteToSiteConn \

—resource-group RG1 \

—query connectionStatus

View peering info:

az network vnet peering list \

—resource-group RG1 \

—vnet-name VNetA

Best Practices

- Use **VNet Peering** within Azure whenever possible for performance and simplicity.
- Design **hub-and-spoke** networks where a central VNet hosts shared services and VPN gateways.
- Use **Gateway Transit** to avoid deploying multiple VPN gateways in each VNet.
- Reserve **/27 or larger** subnets for GatewaySubnet.
- Monitor VPN health with **Azure Monitor** and **Log Analytics**.
- Use **ExpressRoute** for consistent, dedicated connectivity when VPN bandwidth is insufficient.
- Secure VPNs with **IPsec/IKEv2** policies and strong pre-shared keys.

- Tag and document peering relationships and gateway dependencies.

Summary

VNET PEERING AND VPN Gateways are vital tools in building secure, connected Azure environments. Whether linking VNets within Azure or bridging on-premises data centers to the cloud, these features provide flexible, secure, and scalable networking options. By understanding the nuances of their implementation and optimizing connectivity strategies, Azure Administrators can support both cloud-native and hybrid workloads effectively, ensuring continuity, performance, and security across all connected resources.

Monitoring Network Performance

MONITORING NETWORK performance is essential for maintaining the availability, reliability, and security of resources in Azure. A robust monitoring strategy enables administrators to detect anomalies, optimize network paths, troubleshoot bottlenecks, and ensure that the network layer complies with organizational and regulatory policies.

Azure provides a suite of integrated tools under the **Azure Monitor** and **Network Watcher** services, which support metrics collection, diagnostics, packet captures, connection monitoring, topology mapping, and flow logging. Together, these tools form a comprehensive framework for visibility into Azure network performance.

Core Network Monitoring Tools

1. Azure Monitor

AZURE MONITOR COLLECTS and analyzes telemetry data across Azure services. For networking, it supports:

- Network interface metrics
- VPN Gateway metrics
- Load Balancer metrics
- Alerts and dashboards

2. Azure Network Watcher

NETWORK WATCHER PROVIDES deep, packet-level diagnostics and insights. Its key features include:

- **Topology Viewer**
- **IP Flow Verify**
- **Next Hop**
- **Connection Monitor**
- **Packet Capture**
- **NSG Flow Logs**

These tools assist administrators in validating configurations, debugging issues, and optimizing connectivity.

Enabling Network Watcher

NETWORK WATCHER MUST be enabled per region. You can use Azure CLI:

az network watcher configure \

—resource-group MyResourceGroup \

—locations uksouth \

—enabled true

Check the status:

az network watcher list—query "[].{Name:name, Enabled:enabled}"—output table

---

Viewing Network Topology

TOPOLOGY VIEW PROVIDES a visual map of resources in a virtual network, helping administrators understand relationships between VMs, NICs, subnets, and gateways.

Generate topology:

az network watcher show-topology \

—location uksouth \

—resource-group MyResourceGroup

This command returns a JSON map which can be viewed in Azure Portal.

Connection Monitor

CONNECTION MONITOR validates whether a source VM or resource can connect to a target endpoint. It supports continuous monitoring and reporting of connection health and latency.

Step 1: Create a Connection Monitor

AZ NETWORK WATCHER connection-monitor create \

—name WebToDBMonitor \

—resource-group MyResourceGroup \

—location uksouth \

—source-resource /subscriptions/.../resourceGroups/MyResourceGroup/providers/Microsoft.Compute/virtualMachines/WebVM \

—destination-address 10.0.3.4 \

—destination-port 1433

Step 2: Start Monitoring

AZ NETWORK WATCHER connection-monitor start \

—location uksouth \

—name WebToDBMonitor \

—resource-group MyResourceGroup

Monitor results can be viewed in the Azure Portal or queried programmatically.

Packet Capture

PACKET CAPTURE ALLOWS for low-level troubleshooting by capturing traffic on a virtual machine's NIC.

Step 1: Create a Packet Capture Session

AZ NETWORK WATCHER packet-capture create \

—name CaptureSession1 \

—resource-group MyResourceGroup \

—vm WebVM \

—storage-account mystorageacct \

—filters '[{"protocol": "TCP", "remotePort": "443"}]'

Step 2: Stop and Download Capture

AZ NETWORK WATCHER packet-capture stop \

—name CaptureSession1 \

—resource-group MyResourceGroup

Captured data is stored in Azure Blob storage and can be downloaded for analysis in tools like Wireshark.

NSG Flow Logs

NSG FLOW LOGS RECORD information about traffic allowed or denied by security rules. Logs are stored in a storage account and can be processed using Azure Monitor or custom analytics pipelines.

Enable Flow Logs

AZ NETWORK WATCHER flow-log configure \

—nsg WebNSG \

—resource-group MyResourceGroup \

—storage-account mystorageacct \

—enabled true \

—retention 30

Analyze Logs with Traffic Analytics

TRAFFIC ANALYTICS PROCESSES NSG flow logs to visualize traffic patterns and detect anomalies.

Enable via Azure Portal:

1. Go to **Network Watcher > Traffic Analytics.**
2. Select storage account and log workspace.
3. Enable and configure frequency and retention.

Load Balancer Metrics

AZURE LOAD BALANCER provides health and usage metrics through Azure Monitor:

- **Data Path Availability**
- **DipAvailability** (per backend instance)
- **SnatConnectionCount**

- **ByteCount**
- **PacketCount**

Enable metrics collection:

az monitor metrics list \

—resource /subscriptions/<sub-id>/resourceGroups/MyResourceGroup/providers/Microsoft.Network/loadBalancers/MyLB \

—metric DipAvailability

These metrics help validate load distribution and identify underperforming backend instances.

VPN Gateway and ExpressRoute Metrics

VPN GATEWAYS EMIT METRICS like:

- Tunnel status
- Egress and ingress throughput
- P2S connections count

Use metrics to trigger alerts:

az monitor metrics alert create \

—name VPNDisconnectAlert \

—resource-group MyResourceGroup \

—scopes /subscriptions/.../providers/Microsoft.Network/virtualNetworkGateways/MyVPNGateway \

```
—condition "avg TunnelStatus < 1" \
—window-size 5m \
—evaluation-frequency 1m \
—action-group NotifyAdmins
```

Best Practices for Network Monitoring

- Enable **Network Watcher** in all regions with deployed VNets.
- Use **Connection Monitor** for inter-service health checks.
- Schedule **Packet Captures** only when needed—monitoring continuously is costly.
- Enable **NSG Flow Logs** with appropriate retention.
- Store logs in a central **Log Analytics Workspace** for correlation.
- Use **Azure Monitor Alerts** for proactive notifications.
- Analyze flow logs with **Traffic Analytics** to understand normal vs. anomalous patterns.
- Track **Load Balancer** and **VPN** metrics for performance tuning.
- Use **Workbooks** in Azure Monitor for visualizing key network indicators.

Advanced: Integrating with Azure Sentinel

FOR SECURITY-DRIVEN network monitoring, integrate NSG Flow Logs, Firewall Logs, and diagnostics into **Microsoft Sentinel**:

```
az monitor diagnostic-settings create \

—resource /subscriptions/.../resourceGroups/MyResourceGroup/providers/Microsoft.Network/networkSecurityGroups/WebNSG \

—workspace "/subscriptions/.../resourceGroups/logsRG/providers/Microsoft.OperationalInsights/workspaces/SentinelWorkspace" \

—name NSGDiagSentinel \

—logs '[{"category": "NetworkSecurityGroupFlowEvent", "enabled": true}]'
```

This enables advanced threat detection and automated investigation based on network telemetry.

Summary

NETWORK PERFORMANCE monitoring in Azure is an essential practice for diagnosing issues, optimizing throughput, and ensuring the security of workloads. Through tools like Network Watcher, Azure Monitor, and Traffic Analytics, administrators gain full visibility into the behavior of traffic flows, endpoint connectivity, and rule effectiveness. By implementing these tools strategically, organizations ensure their Azure network infrastructure remains healthy, secure, and performant under all operational conditions.

Chapter 6: Monitoring and Backing Up Azure Resources

Configuring Azure Monitor and Alerts

AZURE MONITOR IS A fully integrated, native platform service that delivers a comprehensive solution for collecting, analyzing, and acting on telemetry data from your Azure and on-premises environments. It plays a critical role in observing the health, performance, and availability of your infrastructure and applications. As an Azure Administrator, configuring Azure Monitor and setting up alerts is essential for proactive management and operational excellence.

This section covers the architecture, setup, and configuration of Azure Monitor, as well as the various types of alerts available, including metric, log, and activity log alerts. We will also explore best practices and common use cases for monitoring compute, networking, storage, and PaaS services in Azure.

Core Components of Azure Monitor

AZURE MONITOR PROVIDES:

- **Metrics**: Numeric values describing system state and performance (e.g., CPU usage).
- **Logs**: Structured data from Azure resources, VMs, applications, and diagnostics.
- **Alerts**: Rules that trigger based on metrics or logs.

- **Dashboards**: Visualizations and workbooks for analysis.

- **Autoscale**: Automatically increases or decreases resources based on performance.

These components are integrated with services like Log Analytics, Application Insights, and Azure Automation for full observability.

Enabling Azure Monitor

AZURE MONITOR IS ENABLED by default for most services. To extend its capabilities:

1. **Enable diagnostics** on VMs, load balancers, storage accounts, and other resources.
2. **Connect resources to a Log Analytics Workspace** for log ingestion and querying.
3. **Configure metrics and alert rules** based on business thresholds.

Step 1: Create a Log Analytics Workspace

AZ MONITOR LOG-ANALYTICS workspace create \

—resource-group MyResourceGroup \

—workspace-name MyLogWorkspace \

—location uksouth

Step 2: Enable Diagnostics on a VM

AZ MONITOR DIAGNOSTIC-settings create \

—resource "/subscriptions/<sub-id>/resourceGroups/MyResourceGroup/providers/Microsoft.Compute/virtualMachines/MyVM" \

—workspace "/subscriptions/<sub-id>/resourceGroups/MyResourceGroup/providers/Microsoft.OperationalInsights/workspaces/MyLogWorkspace" \

—name "VMLogging" \

—logs '[{"category": "PerformanceCounters", "enabled": true}]'

Configuring Metrics Collection

AZURE SERVICES EMIT platform metrics by default. Examples:

- **Virtual Machines**: Percentage CPU, Disk Read/Write, Network In/Out
- **Azure SQL**: DTU consumption, Deadlocks
- **App Service**: Requests, Response Time

View metrics:

az monitor metrics list \

—resource /subscriptions/<sub-id>/resourceGroups/MyResourceGroup/providers/Microsoft.Compute/virtualMachines/MyVM \

—metric "Percentage CPU"

Use these metrics to define alerting conditions.

Setting Up Alerts

ALERTS ALLOW YOU TO act on abnormal conditions or events.

Types of Alerts

Alert Type	Triggered By	Use Case
Metric Alert	Numeric threshold	CPU > 80%, Disk latency > 20ms
Log Alert	Query result	Failed login count > 10 in 5 mins
Activity Log	Azure resource events	VM stopped, resource deleted
Prometheus	Container metrics	AKS cluster integrations

Creating a Metric Alert

```
AZ MONITOR METRICS alert create \

—name HighCPUAlert \

—resource-group MyResourceGroup \

—scopes "/subscriptions/<sub-id>/resourceGroups/MyResourceGroup/providers/Microsoft.Compute/virtualMachines/MyVM" \

—condition "avg Percentage CPU > 80" \

—description "High CPU usage alert" \

—window-size 5m \

—evaluation-frequency 1m \

—action-group NotifyAdmins
```

Creating a Log Alert

LOG ALERTS USE **Kusto Query Language (KQL)** and trigger based on the result of a query.

Sample Query: Failed Logins

```
SIGNINLOGS

| where ResultType == "50074"

| summarize Count = count() by bin(TimeGenerated, 5m)

| where Count > 10
```

Create the alert via Azure Portal or ARM template with evaluation criteria.

Activity Log Alerts

ACTIVITY LOG ALERTS track changes to Azure resources, such as VM deletions or modifications to NSGs.

```
az monitor activity-log alert create \

—name "VMDeleteAlert" \

—resource-group MyResourceGroup \

—scopes /subscriptions/<sub-id> \

—condition "category=Administrative and operationName=Delete Virtual Machine" \

—action-group NotifyAdmins
```

Action Groups

ACTION GROUPS DEFINE **what to do** when an alert fires.

Supported actions:

- Email/SMS/Push/Voice
- Azure Function
- Logic App
- Webhook
- ITSM connector

Create action group:

```
az monitor action-group create \
—name NotifyAdmins \
—resource-group MyResourceGroup \
—short-name alertGrp \
—email-receivers name=OpsTeam email=ops@example.com
```

Integrating Azure Monitor with Dashboards

CREATE VISUAL DASHBOARDS using **Azure Monitor Workbooks** to correlate metrics and logs.

- View high CPU VMs
- Network throughput trends

- Alert timelines

Sample dashboard components:

- Grid tables
- Time-series charts
- KPIs
- Heatmaps

You can export workbooks as ARM templates for reuse across environments.

Monitoring Best Practices

- Set **alerts on mission-critical resources** using fine-tuned thresholds.
- Combine **metrics and logs** for broader visibility.
- Use **action groups** to automate remediation (restart VM, scale app, etc.).
- Tag alerts and group by environment for clarity.
- Regularly review **alert noise and tuning**.
- Store logs in a **Log Analytics Workspace** for up to 2 years.
- Use **Scheduled Queries** to detect unusual patterns (e.g., excessive outbound traffic).

- Correlate **alerts with change tracking** and update events.

Cost Considerations

AZURE MONITOR INCURS charges for:

- Ingested data to Log Analytics (per GB)
- Retention beyond 31 days
- Alerts (number of checks, frequency)
- Dashboards and workbooks (no charge)

Optimize costs by:

- Filtering diagnostics to only needed metrics
- Aggregating alerts
- Using basic logs for infrequent queries

Common Use Cases

1. **CPU Threshold Alerts for VMs**

—ALERT IF CPU > 90% for 5 minutes

—use action group to notify admin and restart service

1. **Monitor Web App Availability**

- Metric: HTTP 5xx errors > 1%

- Response time > 2 seconds

1. **Log Alert for Azure AD Sign-in Risk**

SigninLogs

| where RiskLevel == "High"

| summarize count() by UserPrincipalName

1. **Activity Log Alert for NSG Changes**

- Track changes to rule sets for compliance

Summary

AZURE MONITOR AND ALERTING capabilities form the nerve center of operational observability in the Azure platform. By proactively monitoring infrastructure, analyzing logs, and configuring alerts, administrators can detect issues early, automate responses, and maintain performance and reliability. With the right configuration, Azure Monitor evolves from a visibility tool into a core element of intelligent cloud operations.

Using Log Analytics for Deep Insights

AZURE LOG ANALYTICS is a critical part of Azure Monitor that enables deep visibility into the health and performance of your resources. It allows you to collect, correlate, and analyze data from multiple sources—including Azure resources, on-premises systems, and custom applications—using powerful queries written in Kusto Query Language (KQL). As an Azure Administrator, mastering Log

Analytics empowers you to investigate complex issues, identify optimization opportunities, and enforce security compliance.

This section explores how to configure Log Analytics, write effective queries, visualize and export data, integrate with alerts, and adopt best practices for real-time operational intelligence.

What Is Log Analytics?

LOG ANALYTICS IS A cloud-based service that ingests structured and unstructured telemetry data and enables querying across vast datasets in near real time.

Core capabilities include:

- Centralized log collection from VMs, PaaS, and on-prem resources
- Advanced filtering and data correlation
- Visualizations and dashboards
- Security and compliance auditing
- Integration with alerts, workbooks, and automation

Architecture Overview

LOG ANALYTICS WORKS by connecting **data sources** (like VMs, Azure resources, and custom apps) to a **Log Analytics Workspace**. This workspace stores and indexes the data so it can be queried using KQL.

Component	Description
Workspace	Logical container for logs and metadata
Data Source	VMs, Diagnostic settings, Agents, APIs
Table	Logs stored in structured tables (e.g., Heartbeat, Perf, AzureActivity)
KQL	Query language to retrieve and process data
Viewers/ Consumers	Workbooks, Alerts, Dashboards, Sentinel

Setting Up a Log Analytics Workspace

CREATE A WORKSPACE via CLI:

az monitor log-analytics workspace create \

—resource-group MyResourceGroup \

—workspace-name MyLogWorkspace \

—location uksouth

Link a VM to the workspace:

az monitor diagnostic-settings create \

—name VMLogs \

—resource "/subscriptions/xxx/resourceGroups/MyResourceGroup/providers/Microsoft.Compute/virtualMachines/MyVM" \

—workspace "/subscriptions/xxx/resourceGroups/MyResourceGroup/providers/Microsoft.OperationalInsights/workspaces/MyLogWorkspace"

For on-premises VMs or other clouds, install the **Log Analytics Agent** and link using the workspace ID and key.

Writing Kusto Query Language (KQL) Queries

KQL IS A READ-ONLY query language used in Log Analytics, Application Insights, and Azure Sentinel. It supports filtering, aggregation, joins, and time series operations.

Basic Query: Get VM Heartbeats

```
HEARTBEAT

| where TimeGenerated > ago(1h)

| summarize Count = count() by Computer
```

Filter by Computer and Sort

```
HEARTBEAT

| where Computer == "myvm01"

| summarize HeartbeatCount = count() by bin(TimeGenerated, 5m)

| order by TimeGenerated desc
```

Aggregation: Top CPU Utilization

```
PERF

| where ObjectName == "Processor" and CounterName == "% Processor Time"
```

```
| summarize AvgCPU = avg(CounterValue) by Computer
| order by AvgCPU desc
```

Joining Tables: Failed Logins with Network Traffic

```
SIGNINLOGS
| where ResultType == "50074"
| join kind=inner (
AzureDiagnostics
| where Category == "NetworkSecurityGroupRuleCounter"
) on UserPrincipalName
```

Visualizing Query Results

YOU CAN RENDER DATA directly in Log Analytics or use:

- **Workbooks** for customizable dashboards
- **Azure Dashboards** for cross-service visual summaries
- **Power BI** for advanced data storytelling

Example: Render Chart

```
PERF
| where ObjectName == "LogicalDisk" and CounterName == "% Free Space"
```

| summarize avg(CounterValue) by bin(TimeGenerated, 1h), Computer

| render timechart

Workbooks allow additional interactivity (filters, parameters) and can be exported or shared with teams.

Common Tables in Log Analytics

Table	Description
Heartbeat	Agent health and availability
Perf	VM and OS performance metrics
AzureActivity	Resource-level changes and operations
SigninLogs	Azure AD sign-in information
SecurityEvent	Windows event logs (if enabled)
AppRequests	App Insights telemetry (for web apps/APIs)

EACH TABLE HAS A SCHEMA that can be explored using .show commands or the Log Analytics UI.

Integrating Logs with Alerts

YOU CAN CONVERT ANY KQL query into an alert rule that runs on a schedule and triggers actions.

Example: Alert if CPU is > 90% in the last 5 minutes

Perf

| where ObjectName == "Processor" and CounterName == "% Processor Time"

| where CounterValue > 90

| summarize HighCPU = count() by Computer

Use the Azure Portal to define:

- Threshold (e.g., result count > 0)
- Evaluation frequency
- Action group (email, webhook, Logic App)

Automation and Workflows

COMBINE LOG ANALYTICS with Azure Automation or Logic Apps to:

- Auto-scale resources
- Restart unresponsive VMs
- Tag suspicious users
- Enrich alerts with contextual data

Example: When sign-ins from risky countries are detected, trigger a Logic App to disable accounts.

Log Retention and Export

- Default retention: 30 days (can be increased up to 2 years)
- Export data to Storage Account or Event Hub for long-term archiving

SET RETENTION VIA CLI:

```
az monitor log-analytics workspace update \
```

—resource-group MyResourceGroup \

—workspace-name MyLogWorkspace \

—retention-time 180

Export logs:

az monitor diagnostic-settings create \

—name ExportLogs \

—resource "/subscriptions/.../resourceGroups/rg/providers/Microsoft.Network/networkSecurityGroups/myNSG" \

—workspace "/subscriptions/.../resourceGroups/rg/providers/Microsoft.OperationalInsights/workspaces/MyLogWorkspace" \

—logs '[{"category": "NetworkSecurityGroupFlowEvent", "enabled": true}]'

Security and Access Control

LOG ANALYTICS SUPPORTS:

- **Azure RBAC**: Granular access to workspaces and tables
- **Data masking**: Hide sensitive fields
- **Data access policies**: Enforce who can query what

Use **Table-level RBAC** to isolate data for different teams (e.g., security team vs. developers).

Best Practices

- Centralize logs in a **shared workspace** per environment (e.g., dev, prod).
- Use **descriptive query names** and save them for reuse.
- Index and tag data consistently (e.g., Environment, Application, Region).
- Test queries in the **Log Analytics UI** before converting to alerts.
- Use **custom logs** to ingest application-specific telemetry.
- Combine logs with **metrics and traces** for full-stack observability.
- Enable **Log Analytics Agent Health Checks** to monitor ingestion status.
- Apply **Azure Policies** to enforce diagnostics settings across resources.

Summary

LOG ANALYTICS IS A powerful tool that enables Azure Administrators to extract actionable insights from complex infrastructure and application telemetry. By mastering KQL, setting up automated monitoring, and integrating data across resources, you can proactively detect issues, reduce mean time to resolution (MTTR), and support data-driven decisions. Deep insights, when combined with automation and alerting, turn operational visibility into operational excellence.

Setting Up Azure Backup and Recovery Vaults

PROTECTING DATA AND ensuring recoverability in the event of data loss, corruption, or service disruption is a foundational responsibility for Azure Administrators. Azure Backup offers a scalable, secure, and cost-effective solution for backing up a wide variety of Azure and on-premises workloads, including virtual machines, files, databases, and application workloads. Central to Azure Backup is the **Recovery Services vault**, a logical storage entity that stores backup data, policies, and recovery points.

This section provides comprehensive guidance on setting up Azure Backup, configuring backup policies, deploying Recovery Services vaults, restoring data, and applying best practices for backup management across Azure resources.

What Is Azure Backup?

AZURE BACKUP IS A **Backup as a Service (BaaS)** solution that integrates with native Azure tools and services to provide:

- Agentless and agent-based backups
- Long-term retention
- Application-aware backups (SQL, SAP HANA)
- Incremental and differential backups
- Soft-delete and security features

- Granular restore (full VM, disk, file-level)

Azure Backup is fully managed, eliminates the need for complex infrastructure, and integrates with **Azure Policy**, **Log Analytics**, and **Azure Monitor**.

What Is a Recovery Services Vault?

A RECOVERY SERVICES vault is a storage entity in Azure that holds:

- Backup data for virtual machines and workloads
- Backup policies and schedules
- Configuration metadata
- Recovery points and snapshots

Vaults are **regional resources**, meaning backups are stored in the same region as the source unless configured otherwise. You can deploy multiple vaults for isolation by workload, environment, or compliance boundary.

Creating a Recovery Services Vault

Step 1: Create the Vault

AZ BACKUP VAULT CREATE \

—name MyRecoveryVault \

—resource-group MyResourceGroup \

—location uksouth

Step 2: Set Backup Storage Redundancy

CHOOSE FROM:

- **Locally Redundant Storage (LRS)** – cheaper, lower durability
- **Geo-Redundant Storage (GRS)** – default, cross-region durability
- **Zone-Redundant Storage (ZRS)** – available in specific regions

az backup vault backup-properties set \

—name MyRecoveryVault \

—resource-group MyResourceGroup \

—storage-redundancy GeoRedundant

Enabling Backup for Virtual Machines

AZURE VMS CAN BE PROTECTED using agentless backup integration with Azure Backup.

Step 1: Register the VM

AZ BACKUP PROTECTION enable-for-vm \

—vault-name MyRecoveryVault \

—resource-group MyResourceGroup \

—vm myVM01 \

—policy-name DefaultPolicy

This command links the VM to the backup vault and assigns a default backup policy.

Step 2: Customize the Backup Policy

AZ BACKUP POLICY CREATE \

—name DailyPolicy \

—resource-group MyResourceGroup \

—vault-name MyRecoveryVault \

—policy "$(cat policy.json)"

Sample policy.json:

{

"properties": {

"schedulePolicy": {

"schedulePolicyType": "SimpleSchedulePolicy",

"scheduleRunFrequency": "Daily",

"scheduleRunTimes": ["2024-12-01T02:00:00Z"]

},

"retentionPolicy": {

"retentionPolicyType": "SimpleRetentionPolicy",

"dailySchedule": {

```
"retentionTimes": ["2024-12-01T02:00:00Z"],
"retentionDuration": {
"count": 30,
"durationType": "Days"
}
}
},
"backupManagementType": "AzureIaasVM"
}
}
```

Attach this policy to the VM using:

```
az backup protection backup-now \
—vault-name MyRecoveryVault \
—resource-group MyResourceGroup \
—item-name myVM01 \
—retain-until 2024-12-31T23:59:59Z
```

Monitoring and Managing Backups

AZURE BACKUP INTEGRATES with Azure Monitor to provide alerts and reports.

- **Backup jobs** can be viewed in the Recovery Services vault under *Backup Jobs*

- **Alerts** notify you of job failures or missed backups
- **Reports** offer long-term retention insights and auditability

Enable logging:

```
az monitor diagnostic-settings create \
—name BackupLogs \
—resource "/subscriptions/.../resourceGroups/MyResourceGroup/providers/Microsoft.RecoveryServices/vaults/MyRecoveryVault" \
—workspace "/subscriptions/.../resourceGroups/LogRG/providers/Microsoft.OperationalInsights/workspaces/MyLogWorkspace" \
—logs '[{"category": "AzureBackupReport", "enabled": true}]'
```

Use **Azure Backup Reports** in the portal to visualize success rates, job history, and storage trends.

Performing Restores

AZURE BACKUP SUPPORTS **item-level** and **full VM** restores.

VM Restore

RESTORE THE FULL VM:

```
az backup recoverypoint list \
—vault-name MyRecoveryVault \
—resource-group MyResourceGroup \
```

—container-name iaasvmcontainer;iaasvmcontainerv2;MyVM01 \

—item-name MyVM01

Restore to a new VM:

az backup restore restore-disks \

—vault-name MyRecoveryVault \

—resource-group MyResourceGroup \

—container-name iaasvmcontainer;iaasvmcontainerv2;MyVM01 \

—item-name MyVM01 \

—recovery-point-id <RecoveryPointID> \

—storage-account mystorageaccount \

—target-resource-group MyRecoveryGroup

File-Level Restore

AZURE PORTAL ALLOWS file-level recovery via **Mount and Browse**. A temporary VM disk is mounted to explore and restore individual files without restoring the full VM.

Security Features

- **Soft Delete**: Retains deleted backup data for 14 additional days
- **Multi-User Authorization (MUA)**: Requires secondary approval for critical operations
- **Azure RBAC**: Restrict access to vaults and backups

- **Encrypted Backups**: Data is encrypted in transit and at rest using Storage Service Encryption
- **Immutable Vaults**: Prevents deletion or modification of recovery points

ENABLE SOFT DELETE:

```
az backup vault backup-properties set \
—name MyRecoveryVault \
—resource-group MyResourceGroup \
—soft-delete-feature-state Enabled
```

Advanced Scenarios

- **Azure Files Backup**: Protect file shares natively
- **Azure SQL Backup**: App-aware backup and point-in-time restore
- **SAP HANA Backup**: Certified and workload-aware with log backups
- **Cross-Region Restore**: Available for GRS vaults (read-access secondary region)

Best Practices

- Always test restores for critical systems
- Assign granular roles using Azure RBAC

- Use custom policies tailored to workload recovery point objectives (RPO)
- Enable diagnostics and alerting for operational visibility
- Avoid mixing production and dev backups in the same vault
- Use **tags** for automation and compliance tracking (e.g., {"backup": "daily", "env": "prod"})
- Monitor backup health with Azure Monitor alerts
- Set up periodic audits for recovery vault policies and retention compliance

---

Summary

AZURE BACKUP AND RECOVERY Services vaults form the backbone of resilient and recoverable cloud architectures. They eliminate the complexity of traditional backup solutions, provide rich policy-based automation, and integrate seamlessly with other Azure services. By implementing strong backup strategies, using secure vault configurations, and leveraging automated restore and reporting workflows, Azure Administrators can ensure data durability, regulatory compliance, and rapid recovery in the face of unexpected disruptions.

Automating Responses to Alerts

IN MODERN CLOUD OPERATIONS, proactive incident response is essential for minimizing downtime, reducing manual intervention, and ensuring service reliability. Azure Monitor Alerts can be extended beyond notification-only mechanisms by integrating automated actions that remediate issues, escalate incidents, or trigger complex workflows. This approach enhances your operational resilience and supports self-healing infrastructure patterns.

This section explores how to automate responses to alerts using **action groups**, **Azure Functions**, **Logic Apps**, **Azure Automation**, **ITSM connectors**, and **webhooks**. We also cover use cases, implementation strategies, security considerations, and best practices to enable intelligent, automated operations across your Azure environment.

Action Groups: Foundation for Automation

AN ACTION GROUP IS a collection of actions that are triggered when an alert fires. It is reusable across multiple alerts and supports the following types of actions:

- **Email/SMS/Push/Voice**
- **Azure Function**
- **Logic App**
- **Webhook**
- **Azure Automation Runbook**
- **ITSM Connector**

Create a reusable action group:

```
az monitor action-group create \
```

—name CriticalOpsAG \

—resource-group MyResourceGroup \

—short-name CritOps \

—email-receivers name=DevOpsTeam email=devops@example.com \

—azure-function-receiver name=AutoRestartFunc \

—function-app-resource-id "/subscriptions/.../resourceGroups/MyRG/providers/Microsoft.Web/sites/MyFuncApp" \

—function-name RestartVM

Once created, attach this action group to any metric, log, or activity log alert.

Automating with Azure Functions

AZURE FUNCTIONS ENABLE serverless automation in response to alerts. Example scenarios:

- Restart an unresponsive VM
- Send data to a third-party system
- Log custom metrics
- Clean up resources automatically

Example function: Restart a VM when CPU usage is high

const msRestAzure = require("ms-rest-azure");

```
const ComputeManagementClient = require("azure-arm-compute");

module.exports = async function (context, req) {

const credentials = await msRestAzure.loginWithAppServiceMSI({resource: 'https://management.azure.com/'});

const client = new ComputeManagementClient(credentials, process.env['AZURE_SUBSCRIPTION_ID']);

await client.virtualMachines.restart('MyResourceGroup', 'myVM');

context.log('VM restarted');

};
```

Bind this function to an alert using the azure-function-receiver.

Automating with Logic Apps

LOGIC APPS PROVIDE a visual designer and extensive connectors for automating multi-step workflows.

Use Logic Apps to:

- Integrate with Microsoft Teams, Slack, or ServiceNow
- Call APIs or stored procedures
- Handle conditional workflows (e.g., different actions for different severity levels)
- Log incidents in ITSM systems

Example: Auto-create an incident in ServiceNow for a failed

backup job

1. Create a Logic App
2. Add a trigger: "When an Azure Monitor Alert is triggered"
3. Add an action: "Create Record" in ServiceNow
4. Map alert properties (e.g., severity, description, resource ID)

CONFIGURE ACTION GROUP to use the Logic App:

az monitor action-group create \

—name BackupFailureResponder \

—resource-group MyResourceGroup \

—short-name BckFail \

—logic-app-receiver name=CreateIncident logicAppResourceId="/subscriptions/.../resourceGroups/.../providers/Microsoft.Logic/workflows/CreateBackupIncident"

Using Azure Automation Runbooks

AZURE AUTOMATION SUPPORTS PowerShell and Python runbooks to perform stateful operations.

Use Cases:

- Resize underutilized VMs
- Clean up expired resources
- Sync configurations

- Reset NSG rules
- Rotate secrets

Example: PowerShell runbook to stop VM

```
PARAM (
[string]$resourceGroupName,
[string]$vmName
)
Stop-AzVM -ResourceGroupName $resourceGroupName -Name
$vmName -Force
```

Create a webhook for the runbook and connect it to an action group:

```
az automation runbook webhook create \
—automation-account-name MyAutomation \
—name StopVMHook \
—resource-group MyResourceGroup \
—runbook-name StopVMRunbook \
—expiry-time "2025-01-01T00:00:00Z"
```

Webhooks and Custom Systems

WEBHOOKS ALLOW ALERTS to POST data to external systems, enabling integration with:

- Custom APIs
- SIEM tools (Splunk, ELK)
- Configuration Management Databases (CMDBs)
- Alert routing systems

Webhook payload includes alert details such as:

- Alert name
- Resource ID
- Severity
- Description
- Timestamp

Webhook security can be enhanced with:

- Shared secrets
- IP whitelisting
- Token-based authentication

Webhook configuration:

```
az monitor action-group create \
—name NotifyCMDB \
—resource-group MyResourceGroup \
—short-name CMDB \
```

—webhook-receiver name=CMDBHook uri="https://cmdb.example.com/api/alerts"

ITSM Integration

AZURE MONITOR SUPPORTS direct ITSM integration with tools such as:

- ServiceNow
- System Center Service Manager (SCSM)
- Cherwell
- Provance

Steps to integrate:

1. Register the ITSM Connector from Azure Marketplace
2. Provide system credentials and connection settings
3. Map alert severity and properties to incident fields
4. Attach the ITSM connector to action groups

This allows auto-ticket creation, status updates, and incident resolution tracking directly from Azure Monitor.

Conditional Alert Logic and Suppression

AZURE ALLOWS ADVANCED alert tuning using **alert suppression** and **dynamic thresholds**.

- Suppress repeated alerts using alert cooldown windows
- Avoid alert fatigue with adaptive thresholds

- Define escalation logic via Logic Apps or Function branching

Dynamic threshold example:

```
az monitor metrics alert create \
—name AdaptiveAlert \
—resource-group MyResourceGroup \
—scopes "/subscriptions/.../resourceGroups/MyResourceGroup/providers/Microsoft.Compute/virtualMachines/MyVM" \
—condition "avg Percentage CPU > dynamic" \
—evaluation-frequency 5m \
—window-size 30m \
—action-group CriticalOpsAG
```

Monitoring and Auditing Automated Actions

TRACK ALERT EXECUTIONS through:

- **Activity Logs** (action group executions)
- **Log Analytics** (alert run history)
- **Azure Monitor Alert Rules blade**

Audit automation results using:

- **Logic App run history**
- **Function App invocation logs**

- **Automation runbook job history**

You can correlate alerts with automation success/failure to verify resolution effectiveness and refine logic.

Best Practices

- Use **dedicated action groups** for each automation use case.
- Always include a **notification action** in addition to automated steps.
- Implement **idempotent runbooks** to handle duplicate alert triggers gracefully.
- Secure **webhooks** and **Function Apps** with authentication and logging.
- Use **tags** in Logic Apps and Automation accounts to track ownership and function.
- Regularly **test automation flows** using simulated alerts.
- Enable **alert suppression** where frequent noise is expected.
- Use **dynamic thresholds** for metrics with high variance.

Summary

AUTOMATING RESPONSES to Azure Monitor alerts transforms your cloud operations from reactive to proactive. By leveraging tools like Azure Functions, Logic Apps, and Automation Runbooks, you can reduce incident resolution time, eliminate human error, and improve operational efficiency. Whether restarting VMs, escalating incidents, or remediating misconfigurations, these automation strategies ensure your Azure environment remains resilient, responsive, and intelligent.

Cost Management and Optimization Tools

EFFECTIVE COST MANAGEMENT is a critical responsibility for Azure Administrators and cloud operations teams. With the rise of cloud-native architectures, organizations are consuming an ever-growing portfolio of Azure services, and without proper oversight, costs can escalate rapidly. Azure provides a robust suite of tools designed to give visibility into resource consumption, forecast expenditures, allocate budgets, and implement strategies to control and optimize cloud spending.

This section provides a comprehensive guide to Azure's cost management and optimization features, including how to configure cost alerts, analyze usage data, apply savings plans and reservations, tag and group costs, and automate cost governance using policies and scripting.

Core Tools for Cost Management

AZURE COST MANAGEMENT + Billing is the central hub for tracking, allocating, and optimizing Azure expenditure. It consists of the following components:

- **Cost Analysis:** Visualizes costs by resource, department, project, or tag.

- **Budgets**: Define thresholds and send alerts when nearing or exceeding limits.
- **Recommendations**: Built-in insights for reducing spend.
- **Reservations and Savings Plans**: Commit to usage for discounts.
- **Exports**: Send cost data to storage or external systems.
- **Pricing Calculator and TCO Calculator**: Estimate and compare cost scenarios.

Understanding Azure Billing Structure

BEFORE DIVING INTO tools, it's important to understand how Azure bills services:

- **Pay-As-You-Go**: Metered usage by the second/ minute/hour.
- **Reserved Instances (RIs)**: 1- or 3-year commitment with discount.
- **Savings Plans**: Flexible commitment across multiple resources.
- **Spot Pricing**: Deeply discounted for interruptible workloads.
- **Marketplace Costs**: From third-party publishers.

Each bill includes:

- **Resource-level consumption data**
- **Tax and overage charges**
- **Currency and region-specific pricing**

Setting Up Budgets

BUDGETS ALLOW TEAMS to define cost limits over a defined period (monthly, quarterly, annually) and configure alerts as thresholds are approached or breached.

Create a Budget via CLI

AZ CONSUMPTION BUDGET create \

—amount 2000 \

—budget-name ProjectXMonthlyBudget \

—category cost \

—time-grain monthly \

—start-date 2024-06-01 \

—end-date 2025-06-01 \

—resource-group MyResourceGroup \

—notifications '[{"enabled": true, "operator": "GreaterThan", "threshold": 80, "contactEmails": ["team@example.com"]}]'

Budgets are non-enforcing—they notify but don't restrict spend. Enforcement can be layered via Azure Policies or custom automation.

Cost Analysis and Forecasting

COST ANALYSIS ENABLES the visualization of accrued and forecasted costs using flexible filters and groupings:

- **Filter by**: Subscription, resource group, resource type, tag, location
- **Group by**: Service name, meter category, cost center
- **View types**: Daily, monthly, forecast, amortized

Use the portal: **Cost Management > Cost Analysis**

To automate cost analysis:

az consumption usage list \

—start-date 2024-05-01 \

—end-date 2024-05-31 \

—query "[].{Resource:instanceName, Cost:pretaxCost, Service:meterDetails.meterName}"

Export results to Excel/CSV or ingest into Power BI for advanced analysis.

Scheduling Cost Exports

YOU CAN SCHEDULE REGULAR exports of cost data to an Azure Storage account.

az costmanagement export create \

—name MyMonthlyExport \

—scope "/subscriptions/xxxx" \

—type Usage \

—time-frame MonthToDate \

—recurrence Monthly \

—recurrence-period "start=2024-01-01T00:00:00Z;end=2025-01-01T00:00:00Z" \

—storage-account-id "/subscriptions/.../resourceGroups/rg/providers/Microsoft.Storage/storageAccounts/mystorage" \

—container mystoragecontainer \

—file-format Csv

These files can be integrated into BI pipelines or financial reporting systems.

Cost Alerts and Notifications

ALERTS PROVIDE REAL-time visibility into unexpected changes or trends in spending.

Types of cost alerts:

- **Budget alerts**: Triggered based on budget thresholds.
- **Anomaly detection**: Based on usage pattern deviation.
- **Price changes**: From Azure or marketplace publishers.

Enable anomaly detection:

az advisor recommendation enable \

—name CostAnomalyDetection \

—scope "/subscriptions/xxxx"

Integrate alerts with **Action Groups** to route messages to email, SMS, or automation workflows.

Reservations and Savings Plans

AZURE RESERVATIONS provide cost savings (up to 72%) by pre-paying for one-year or three-year usage commitments.

Eligible services:

- Virtual Machines
- Azure SQL Database
- Cosmos DB
- App Service Plans

Purchase via Portal: **Cost Management > Reservations**

Or via CLI:

az reservations reservation-order purchase \

—sku Standard_D2s_v3 \

—quantity 1 \

—term P1Y \

—billing-scope-id "/subscriptions/xxxx"

Savings Plans offer flexibility across resource types within compute category, optimizing price without binding to a single SKU.

Using Azure Advisor for Recommendations

AZURE ADVISOR ANALYZES deployed services and provides actionable recommendations across four areas:

- **Cost**
- **Security**
- **Performance**
- **Operational Excellence**

Example cost recommendations:

- Resize underutilized VMs
- Remove unattached disks or unused IPs
- Replace pay-as-you-go with reservations
- Enable auto-shutdown for dev/test VMs

Query recommendations:

az advisor recommendation list—category Cost

These insights are periodically updated and can be exported or embedded in workflows.

Tagging for Chargeback and Cost Allocation

TAGS ENABLE GROUPING resources by business unit, application, environment, or cost center.

Apply a tag:

az tag create—resource-id /subscriptions/xxxx/resourceGroups/MyRG/providers/Microsoft.Compute/virtualMachines/myVM—tags Department=Finance Environment=Prod

Use tags in cost analysis:

- View cost by tag (e.g., Department, Project)
- Allocate shared costs (e.g., networking, identity)
- Support internal chargebacks or showbacks

Governance with Azure Policy

AZURE POLICY ENSURES compliance with cost-saving configurations:

- Enforce VM SKU restrictions (e.g., no high-cost instances in dev)
- Require shutdown schedules
- Enforce tagging standards
- Block creation of unapproved services

Example: Policy to require a tag

```
{
"if": {
"field": "tags['CostCenter']",
"equals": null
```

```
},
"then": {
"effect": "deny"
}
}
```

Assign policy via:

```
az policy assignment create \
—policy "RequireCostCenterTag" \
—name "CostTagEnforcement" \
—scope "/subscriptions/xxxx"
```

Automating Optimization

COMBINE ALERTS, POLICIES, and scripts to enforce cost hygiene:

- Schedule cleanup of idle resources
- Auto-shutdown for non-prod VMs
- Archive cold storage data
- Resize underused VMs weekly

Use **Azure Automation**, **Logic Apps**, or **Functions** for implementation.

Best Practices

- Define budgets for each **environment** and **project**.
- Regularly review **Advisor recommendations**.
- Use **tags** consistently across all resources.
- Track shared resources separately and allocate via tags or cost models.
- Choose **Reservations or Savings Plans** for predictable workloads.
- Avoid orphaned resources (NICs, disks, public IPs).
- Monitor **daily spend trends** for anomalies.
- Educate teams with **self-service dashboards** in Azure Portal or Power BI.

Summary

AZURE COST MANAGEMENT and optimization tools empower organizations to control, predict, and reduce cloud spending. By leveraging budgets, tagging strategies, automated exports, and intelligent recommendations, Azure Administrators can ensure efficient resource usage, support financial accountability, and align cloud operations with business goals. Integrating cost governance into your operational workflows ensures scalability is matched with sustainability—financially and operationally.

Chapter 7: Preparing for the AZ-104 Exam

Study Plan and Exam Strategy

SUCCESSFULLY PASSING the AZ-104: Microsoft Azure Administrator certification requires more than just familiarity with Azure services—it demands a strategic approach to studying, a thorough understanding of exam objectives, and hands-on experience. This section will guide you through constructing a personalized, efficient, and effective study plan while offering proven exam strategies to maximize your chance of success on the first attempt.

We'll break down preparation into phases: planning, studying, practicing, and test execution. Each phase includes practical steps, tools, and schedules that can be adapted based on your background and availability.

Understanding the Exam Scope

THE AZ-104 EXAM TESTS the ability to manage and maintain core Azure services. Microsoft regularly updates the exam blueprint to reflect evolving cloud practices.

Current high-level domains (subject to change):

1. Manage Azure identities and governance (15–20%)
2. Implement and manage storage (15–20%)
3. Deploy and manage Azure compute resources (20–25%)
4. Configure and manage virtual networking (20–25%)
5. Monitor and back up Azure resources (10–15%)

Key expectation: Perform administrator-level tasks, use Azure CLI, PowerShell, and ARM templates, and work with Azure AD, VMs, VNets, and backup/monitoring tools.

Phase 1: Planning and Scheduling

START BY ASSESSING your experience and availability.

Step 1: Self-Assessment

- Do you use Azure in your job?
- Are you familiar with scripting (CLI, PowerShell)?
- Have you deployed VMs, set up VNets, or configured backups?

Step 2: Time Allocation

ALLOCATE TIME BASED on your background:

Experience Level	Study Time	Recommended Duration
Beginner	80–100 hours	6–8 weeks
Intermediate	50–70 hours	4–6 weeks
Advanced	30–50 hours	2–4 weeks

Step 3: Build Your Study Calendar

DIVIDE YOUR STUDY SESSIONS into manageable blocks:

- Week 1–2: Identity & governance + storage
- Week 3–4: Compute + networking

- Week 5: Backup/monitoring + practice tests
- Week 6: Review, revise, and test strategies

Phase 2: Studying Effectively

COMBINE LEARNING METHODS for better retention.

1. Official Documentation

USE MICROSOFT LEARN as your primary resource:

https://learn.microsoft.com/en-us/certifications/exams/az-104

Each module is aligned to an exam objective. Example:

- Manage subscriptions and governance
- Configure VMs and scale sets
- Set up Azure Blob and file storage

2. Books and Study Guides

USE COMPREHENSIVE STUDY materials such as:

- **"Exam Ref AZ-104 Microsoft Azure Administrator"** by Harshul Patel
- This guide (you are reading) – practical, exam-focused, and lab-integrated

3. Labs and Hands-on Practice

USE A **free Azure sandbox** from Microsoft Learn or your personal Azure subscription. Key labs:

- Create Azure AD users, groups, and RBAC roles
- Deploy and manage VMs with CLI and Portal
- Configure VNets, NSGs, and peering
- Set up a Recovery Services vault and run a VM backup
- Configure alerts and dashboards with Azure Monitor

4. Flashcards and Note-Taking

USE FLASHCARD APPS (e.g., Anki, Quizlet) to remember:

- CLI commands and flags
- Service tiers (e.g., storage redundancy types)
- Pricing models and reserved instance scenarios
- Identity features (MFA, roles, hybrid identity)

Keep a notebook or OneNote organized by domain for review.

Phase 3: Practice and Simulation

TESTING UNDER EXAM-like conditions prepares your mind for the real challenge.

Practice Tests

USE REPUTABLE AZ-104 practice tests from:

- MeasureUp (official provider)
- Whizlabs
- Tutorials Dojo
- Microsoft Learn knowledge checks

Track your performance:

- <70%: Review topics in-depth
- 70–85%: Good, but refine weak areas
- 85%: Solid; move on to strategy

Mock Exams

SIMULATE THE REAL TEST:

- Set a 180-minute timer
- Avoid notes or internet
- Review not only wrong answers but also lucky guesses

Phase 4: Exam Strategy

KNOWING HOW TO TAKE the test is as important as what you know.

What to Expect

- 40–60 questions
- Multiple choice, drag-and-drop, case studies
- Scenario-based and interactive questions
- No back button for case studies
- Time: 180 minutes max

Strategy Tips

- **Read the question twice**: Many errors are from misreading, not misunderstanding
- **Eliminate obvious wrong choices**: Increases your odds even if you're unsure
- **Time management**: Don't spend more than 3 minutes per question early on
- **Flag and revisit**: Skip tough ones and come back if time allows
- **Use process of elimination**: Especially on CLI commands or config steps
- **Know when to guess**: No penalties for wrong answers

Tools and Resources

Tool	Purpose	Link
Microsoft Learn	Interactive learning paths	learn.microsoft.com[3]
Azure Free Account	Hands-on practice	azure.microsoft.com/free[4]
Exam Sandbox	Test interface simulation	aka.ms/examdemo
AZ-104 Skills Outline	Updated exam topics	aka.ms/AZ-104skills
Microsoft Learn Labs	Browser-based exercises	microsoft.com/learn-labs[5]
GitHub Lab Repos	Sample Bicep/ARM templates	github.com/Azure[6]

Summary Checklist

- Review official skills outline
- Build a study calendar
- Complete Microsoft Learn modules
- Do 3–5 full-length practice exams
- Achieve consistent 80%+ on mocks
- Perform all key labs hands-on
- Revise weak areas in final week

3. https://learn.microsoft.com/
4. https://azure.microsoft.com/free
5. https://microsoft.com/learn-labs
6. https://github.com/Azure

- Prepare testing environment (quiet, stable internet)
- Sleep well before exam day

Final Thought

CERTIFICATION IS NOT just about passing an exam—it's about validating your ability to perform real-world tasks in a cloud environment. AZ-104 tests both knowledge and execution. With the right plan, disciplined study, and effective test strategy, you'll not only earn the credential but also elevate your skills and value as a professional Azure Administrator.

Practice Questions and Test-Taking Tips

THE AZ-104: MICROSOFT Azure Administrator exam challenges candidates with a mix of technical depth, breadth of knowledge, and real-world scenario understanding. Practicing with representative questions and understanding test-taking strategies can significantly improve both your score and confidence. This section provides an in-depth guide on how to approach exam questions, including a variety of practice scenarios, explanations for each answer, and guidance on how to interpret question styles and apply your knowledge effectively.

We'll explore the common question formats, provide realistic question examples with explanations, and walk through strategies that will help you answer correctly even when you're unsure. The goal is not just to memorize answers but to understand Azure in a way that allows you to apply concepts confidently in exam conditions.

Common AZ-104 Question Formats

THE AZ-104 EXAM CONSISTS of a range of question types, including:

- **Multiple-choice questions** (single or multiple answers)
- **Drag-and-drop matching** (e.g., match service to scenario)
- **Hot area** (select the correct element(s) on a screenshot or diagram)
- **Case studies** (multi-step scenario questions with locked navigation)
- **Yes/No questions** (evaluate the validity of a statement)
- **Fill-in-the-blank style with code or CLI commands**

Understanding these formats will help you manage your time and approach each question strategically.

Sample Practice Questions

Question 1: RBAC and Resource Groups

YOU NEED TO ALLOW A group of developers to create and manage resources within a specific resource group. They should not be allowed to delete the resource group or modify access to it.

Which role should you assign?

A. Contributor

B. Owner

C. User Access Administrator

D. Reader

Answer: A

Explanation: The Contributor role allows creating and managing resources within a resource group but does not allow deleting the group itself or assigning roles. Owner allows all actions including access control. Reader is too limited, and User Access Administrator is focused only on managing access.

Question 2: Azure Storage Replication

YOU ARE DEPLOYING AN application that must comply with local data residency laws. Data must not leave the Azure region where it is created. Which replication option should you choose?

A. GRS

B. RA-GRS

C. ZRS

D. LRS

Answer: D

Explanation: LRS (Locally Redundant Storage) keeps data in a single region and satisfies data residency requirements. GRS and RA-GRS replicate to secondary regions, violating the requirement. ZRS spans availability zones within a region but might replicate metadata outside.

Question 3: VM Scale Sets

YOU MANAGE A STATELESS web app running in a virtual machine scale set. You want to ensure that the app automatically scales based on CPU usage.

What should you do?

A. Configure availability zones

B. Configure autoscale settings

C. Use an availability set

D. Enable accelerated networking

Answer: B

Explanation: To automatically scale a VM scale set, configure autoscale rules based on performance metrics like CPU usage. Availability zones and sets handle fault tolerance, and accelerated networking is a performance optimization unrelated to scaling.

Question 4: CLI Command Evaluation

WHICH AZURE CLI COMMAND creates a virtual network with an address space of 10.0.0.0/16 and a subnet named web using 10.0.1.0/24?

A.

az network vnet create—name myVNet—resource-group myRG—address-prefix 10.0.0.0/16—subnet-name web—subnet-prefix 10.0.1.0/24

B.

az network vnet new—name myVNet—group myRG—ip 10.0.0.0/16—subnet web 10.0.1.0/24

C.

az vnet create—name myVNet—group myRG—address 10.0.0.0/16—sub web 10.0.1.0/24

D.

az vnet new—resource-group myRG—name myVNet—prefix 10.0.0.0/16—subnet-name web

Answer: A

Explanation: Option A correctly uses the Azure CLI syntax for creating a VNet with a defined address space and subnet. Other options are syntactically incorrect or incomplete.

Question 5: Backup Strategy

YOU NEED TO BACK UP a VM daily and retain each backup for 30 days. Which component should you configure?

A. Azure Monitor

B. Recovery Services vault

C. Azure Blob Lifecycle Management

D. Azure Site Recovery

Answer: B

Explanation: Recovery Services vault is used for VM backups. Azure Monitor is for alerts and logs, Blob lifecycle management is for blob data, and Site Recovery is for disaster recovery—not backup.

Tips for Each Question Type

Multiple Choice

- Always **eliminate** obviously incorrect answers first.
- For "Choose two/three" questions, ensure each selected item is valid on its own.
- Watch for **qualifiers** like "must," "only," "best," "first."

Drag-and-Drop

- Practice with common mappings: service → scenario, tier → feature, tool → task.
- Understand subtle differences (e.g., Azure Policy vs. Azure Blueprints).

Case Studies

- Read the **last question first** to know what you're looking for.
- Use the information panel efficiently—don't reread everything each time.
- Navigate **strategically**—you cannot go back once you move forward.

Yes/No Questions

- These often test edge case understanding. If a config setting is not default or requires enabling, the answer is often "No."
- Double-check for **implicit requirements** like permission scope or SKU.

Time Management During Exam

- Allocate roughly **2.5–3 minutes per question**.
- Flag and skip questions that are unclear—mark for review.
- Case studies often come at the end and **do not allow backtracking**—budget at least 20–30 minutes for them.

Recommended Study Resources for Practice

Resource	Description
Microsoft Learn	Free knowledge checks, official modules
MeasureUp	Official practice tests with detailed feedback
Tutorials Dojo (Jon Bonso)	Known for tough, realistic scenarios
ExamTopics	Community-sourced questions and discussion
Whizlabs	Practice exams with explanations
GitHub - AzureExamRepo	Hands-on labs and scenario simulations

Simulation and Recall Techniques

- **Use flashcards** for CLI syntax, role definitions, feature limits.
- Practice **brain dumps ethically**: Write down services, ports, roles, regions at start of exam (memory dump sheet).
- Use **mind maps** to connect services (e.g., how NSG interacts with subnet/VNet).

Pitfalls to Avoid

- **Relying solely on memorization** instead of hands-on practice.
- Misunderstanding **default behavior** (e.g., NSG rules, public IPs).

- Ignoring **constraints or limitations** (e.g., VM sizes in availability zones).
- Overlooking **service tiers and SKUs**—many answers hinge on this detail.

Summary

PRACTICE QUESTIONS provide insight into Microsoft's testing methodology and reinforce your technical knowledge in a realistic context. To succeed in AZ-104, simulate the exam environment, mix question formats during revision, and don't just memorize—focus on **why** the right answer works. By understanding how Azure services operate and interact, and by refining your test-taking strategies, you equip yourself not only to pass the exam but to function effectively as a certified Azure Administrator in the field.

Common Pitfalls and How to Avoid Them

ACHIEVING SUCCESS IN the AZ-104: Microsoft Azure Administrator exam goes beyond understanding services and syntax—it requires anticipating and avoiding the common mistakes that derail even well-prepared candidates. These pitfalls often arise not from a lack of knowledge, but from misinterpretation of questions, overlooking small details, or poor exam strategy.

This section identifies the most frequent exam-day and preparation-related mistakes observed among AZ-104 candidates and provides concrete strategies for how to avoid them. By learning from these insights, you'll be better equipped to stay focused, accurate, and confident under exam pressure.

Pitfall 1: Underestimating the Exam Scope

PROBLEM: Candidates often focus heavily on compute or networking topics and neglect others like governance, cost control, or Azure Monitor.

Symptoms:

- You've never used Azure Policy or Blueprints.
- You skip identity management because it's "not real admin work."
- You've never configured budgets or diagnostic settings.

Avoidance Strategy:

- Follow the official skills outline (download from Microsoft's website).
- Map each study session to a percentage weight of the exam (e.g., Networking = 25%).
- Use the "weakest first" study principle: spend more time on domains you are least familiar with.

Pitfall 2: Memorizing Without Context

PROBLEM: Relying on rote memorization of command-line flags or service limits without understanding how they apply in real-world scenarios.

Symptoms:

- You remember the flag—assign-identity but not when to use it.
- You can recite NSG rule priorities but don't know how they affect VM connectivity.
- You're thrown off by slight wording changes in questions.

Avoidance Strategy:

- Practice tasks in the Azure Portal, CLI, or Bicep before reviewing flashcards.
- Use CLI documentation and man pages to understand options.
- Create real-life labs: Deploy a VM with backup and monitoring from scratch.

Pitfall 3: Ignoring Question Structure and Keywords

PROBLEM: Many questions are scenario-based with subtle qualifiers like "must," "first," "best," or "only," which drastically change what the correct answer is.

Symptoms:

- Missing "select two answers" instructions.
- Choosing a correct option that doesn't fulfill all conditions in the question.

- Misidentifying what the question is truly asking (e.g., operational task vs. governance goal).

Avoidance Strategy:

- Read the question twice. First for context, second for specifics.
- Highlight qualifiers (mentally or physically if allowed).
- Eliminate options that only partially meet the requirement.

Pitfall 4: Mismanaging Time During the Exam

PROBLEM: Spending too much time on early questions or case studies, leaving little time to complete or review the rest of the exam.

Symptoms:

- You complete only 60% of the questions before the timer gets to 15 minutes.
- You feel rushed during the last third of the exam.
- You fail to return to flagged questions due to time pressure.

Avoidance Strategy:

- Stick to a strict time-per-question rule: ~2.5 minutes/question.
- Don't obsess over a single tricky scenario. Flag it and return.

- Save 25–30 minutes at the end for case studies if they are at the end of the exam.

Pitfall 5: Overlooking Default Behaviors and Limits

PROBLEM: Candidates often assume custom configurations rather than knowing default settings, leading to incorrect answers.

Examples:

- NSG rules are deny-all by default unless explicitly allowed.
- Public IPs are not assigned to VMs unless requested.
- Storage accounts are encrypted by default using Microsoft-managed keys.

Avoidance Strategy:

- Focus on "out-of-the-box" behaviors during your revision.
- Review documentation for default values, limits, and behaviors.
- Use Microsoft Learn "knowledge checks" that emphasize defaults.

Pitfall 6: Confusing Azure Services with Similar Names

PROBLEM: Azure has multiple services that sound similar but serve different purposes (e.g., Azure Backup vs. Azure Site Recovery).

Examples:

- Confusing Azure Monitor with Log Analytics or Azure Advisor.
- Mixing up Azure Policy and Azure RBAC.
- Assuming Azure Automation and Azure Logic Apps are interchangeable.

Avoidance Strategy:

- Create a comparison table of similar services.
- Use side-by-side documentation or portal navigation to identify differences.
- Make quick reference flashcards: "Azure Backup → data protection; ASR → DR replication."

Pitfall 7: Overreliance on the Portal

PROBLEM: Candidates use only the Azure Portal and avoid CLI, PowerShell, or ARM/Bicep templates during study. The exam includes syntax-based questions and automation-related scenarios.

Symptoms:

- CLI syntax questions seem foreign.
- You don't recognize az role assignment or az network nsg rule create.
- Infrastructure-as-Code tasks are confusing.

Avoidance Strategy:

- Run every Portal task in CLI at least once.
- Practice deploying with ARM templates or Bicep using sandbox environments.
- Review the most common CLI commands and their use cases.

Pitfall 8: Skipping Governance and Compliance Topics

PROBLEM: Governance tools like Azure Policy, Cost Management, Blueprints, and Tags are often skipped because they seem less "technical."

Symptoms:

- Not understanding how tags affect cost analysis.
- Unable to distinguish Azure Policy from RBAC.
- Forgetting that budgets don't enforce spending caps.

Avoidance Strategy:

- Spend dedicated time on Cost Management, Azure Policy, and tagging.
- Create mock compliance scenarios and apply policies.
- Use Azure Advisor's governance recommendations as a study guide.

Pitfall 9: Using Outdated Study Materials

PROBLEM: Azure changes frequently, and many exam questions reflect current behavior and UI, making outdated material dangerous.

Symptoms:

- Answers based on classic deployments or deprecated services.
- CLI commands that no longer work.
- Confusion due to differences in screenshots or parameter names.

Avoidance Strategy:

- Always check the publication date of guides and courses.
- Cross-reference with Microsoft Learn and Docs.
- Subscribe to Azure updates or use changelogs.

Pitfall 10: Exam Day Unpreparedness

PROBLEM: Many otherwise ready candidates underperform due to poor preparation for the exam environment itself.

Symptoms:

- Browser crashes or hardware issues during online proctored exams.
- Nervousness or distractions during testing.
- Failing identity verification due to lighting, noise, or document issues.

Avoidance Strategy:

- Test your system early if taking the exam online.
- Choose a quiet room with stable internet.
- Bring valid ID, and prepare a clean desk space.
- Sleep well and arrive early to reduce anxiety.

Summary Checklist

AVOIDING COMMON PITFALLS is just as important as mastering the content. Use this quick checklist:

- Studied all exam domains, not just compute and networking
- Practiced both CLI and Portal tasks

- Understood default settings and service limits
- Created comparison sheets for similar services
- Simulated exam conditions during practice
- Avoided relying solely on memorization
- Studied updated materials from trusted sources
- Practiced time management with a question timer
- Reviewed tricky areas like governance, RBAC, and backups
- Prepared your environment for exam day (online or test center)

Final Thought

MOST CANDIDATES WHO fail the AZ-104 exam do so not because of a lack of knowledge, but because of poor planning, skipped topics, or simple misinterpretations. Avoiding these pitfalls can dramatically improve your confidence, accuracy, and final score. Combine strong foundational knowledge with disciplined exam technique, and you'll be well on your way to Azure Administrator certification success.

Mind Maps and Cheat Sheets

MIND MAPS AND CHEAT sheets are powerful tools for consolidating complex information into digestible, visual formats that reinforce learning and facilitate rapid review. For the AZ-104: Microsoft Azure Administrator exam, which encompasses a broad spectrum of services and administrative responsibilities, well-organized visual references can dramatically enhance recall, especially in high-pressure testing environments.

This section presents structured guidance on how to create and use mind maps and cheat sheets to aid AZ-104 preparation. It covers subject-specific breakdowns, templates for each exam domain, prioritized facts, and tips on integrating these resources into your daily study routine.

Benefits of Mind Maps and Cheat Sheets

- **Visual summarization**: Helps link related topics and concepts through associations.

- **Quick revision**: Useful for last-minute reviews before the exam.

- **Memory reinforcement**: Colors, structure, and connections aid long-term retention.

- **Gap identification**: Quickly reveals areas where understanding is weak or incomplete.

- **Customizability**: Adaptable to your learning style and preferences.

How to Create an Effective Mind Map

1. **Start from core domains**: Use the five AZ-104 skill areas as your main branches.
2. **Break down each domain** into services, tools, commands, and scenarios.

3. **Use color coding**: Assign unique colors to each domain for visual segmentation.
4. **Add quick notes or commands**: Write minimal but functional syntax.
5. **Use digital tools**: Apps like XMind, MindMeister, or draw.io help create scalable maps.
6. **Keep it to 1–2 pages per domain** to maintain usability.

Sample Mind Map Structure

Domain: Manage Azure Identities and Governance

- **Azure AD**

○ Users

○ Groups

○ Service Principals

○ Hybrid Identity (AD Connect)

- **RBAC**

○ Built-in roles: Owner, Contributor, Reader, etc.

○ Custom roles

○ Scope: Management Group > Subscription > RG > Resource

- **Azure Policy**

○ Policy Definitions

- Initiatives
- Effects: audit, deny, append

- **Management Groups**
  - Hierarchy
  - Inheritance

Add Note:

- az role assignment create—assignee user@example.com—role Reader—scope /subscriptions/...

Example Cheat Sheet: Networking Commands

NSG

- Create:

az network nsg create—name MyNSG—resource-group MyRG

- Add rule:

az network nsg rule create—nsg-name MyNSG—name AllowHTTP—priority 100—direction Inbound—access Allow—protocol Tcp—destination-port-range 80—source-address-prefix Internet

VNet Peering

- Create peering:

az network vnet peering create—name LinkAtoB—resource-group MyRG—vnet-name VNetA—remote-vnet VNetB—allow-vnet-access

---

Core Areas to Include in Cheat Sheets

1. Identity and Access

- RBAC role hierarchy
- Azure AD vs AAD DS
- Conditional Access policy purpose
- Azure MFA configuration

2. Storage

- Storage tiers (Hot, Cool, Archive)
- Redundancy types (LRS, ZRS, GRS)
- Shared access signature (SAS) types
- Storage account firewall and networking settings

3. Compute

- VM size families and use cases
- Availability Sets vs Zones

- VMSS scaling rules
- Backup requirements (Recovery Services vault)

4. Networking

- NSG default rules
- VNet peering and gateway transit
- Route table (UDR) behavior
- DNS resolution options

5. Monitoring and Backup

- Azure Monitor alert types
- Log Analytics tables (Perf, Heartbeat, SigninLogs)
- Backup retention options
- Soft delete and MUA settings

6. Automation and Governance

- Policy effects
- Initiative vs Policy definition
- Blueprint lifecycle
- Cost Management: Budgets, exports, tags

Mind Map Examples by Domain

Compute Domain

- **VM Types**
  - D-series (general)
  - E-series (memory)
  - F-series (compute)
- **Scaling**
  - VMSS vs Availability Set
  - Autoscale rules
- **Images**
  - Marketplace
  - Custom managed images
- **Backup**
  - Vault → Policy → Backup Item

Storage Domain

- **Account Types**
  - General Purpose v2
  - BlobStorage

- **Security**
  - SAS
  - Private Endpoints
  - Azure AD integration
- **Lifecycle Management**
  - Rules for tiering or deletion

Sample Fast Facts for Revision

Topic	Key Fact
NSG Rules	Default rules deny all unless allowed
Storage Tier	Archive = offline, needs rehydration
Availability Set	Update + Fault domain redundancy
RBAC Scope	Always assign at the lowest effective scope
Azure Policy	Audit or deny non-compliant deployments
Budget Alerts	Notify, but do not enforce limits
Log Retention	Log Analytics: 30-day default, configurable
DNS Resolution	Azure DNS or custom DNS per VNet

Incorporating Into Study Schedule

- **Daily quick review**: Spend 10 minutes per day reviewing one domain mind map.
- **Print for offline use**: Keep cheat sheets on your desk for spontaneous revision.

- **Use before practice tests**: Review critical sheets before attempting practice exams.
- **Memory dump**: Memorize top 10 facts or commands to "brain dump" at the start of the exam.

Tools to Create Mind Maps & Cheat Sheets

Tool	Use Case	Notes
XMind	Detailed mind map creation	Free + Pro version available
draw.io	Browser-based, integrates with Google	Free, flexible templates
Notion	Organizing markdown-style cheat notes	Great for connected concepts
Obsidian	Offline markdown + linking	Powerful for long-form cheat sheets
Anki	Spaced-repetition for flashcard recall	Add command-line flags, limits, syntax

Summary

MIND MAPS AND CHEAT sheets serve as the backbone of efficient review and retention strategies for AZ-104. They condense sprawling documentation and real-world scenarios into concise, structured formats that support focused learning and rapid recall. As you approach your exam date, these tools will help you sharpen your memory, reinforce weak spots, and stay confident in your knowledge. Used properly, they can make the difference between just passing and excelling.

Chapter 8: Excelling as an Azure Administrator Beyond Certification

Real-World Admin Scenarios and Best Practices

EARNING THE AZ-104 certification marks the beginning—not the end—of your journey as an Azure Administrator. Real-world success depends on your ability to apply foundational knowledge to practical scenarios, make architectural decisions under pressure, and maintain operational excellence in fast-paced cloud environments. Whether you're working solo or as part of a large team, you'll be expected to manage costs, enforce security, scale services, troubleshoot performance, and maintain compliance.

This section focuses on real-world administrative scenarios and proven best practices. It draws from actual use cases that Azure professionals encounter daily—spanning identity management, compute operations, storage, networking, automation, and incident response. Through these examples, you'll learn how to elevate your operational skill set from certified technician to trusted administrator.

Scenario 1: Enforcing Least Privilege Access with RBAC

CHALLENGE: Your company wants to ensure that junior developers can deploy web apps but cannot modify virtual networks or access secrets.

Approach:

1. Use Azure AD groups: DevWebTeam, NetAdmins,

SecOps.
2. Assign the **Web Contributor** role to the DevWebTeam scoped only to the AppService-RG.
3. Assign **Key Vault Reader** to SecOps, and no access for developers.
4. Assign **Network Contributor** only to NetAdmins.

Best Practice:

- Always assign roles at the **lowest effective scope** (resource group > resource).
- Use **custom roles** if built-in roles are too permissive.
- Document and review role assignments monthly.

Scenario 2: High Availability Design for a Production Web Application

CHALLENGE: You need to deploy a public-facing web app that must have 99.99% availability.

Approach:

1. Deploy the app across **two or more Availability Zones** in a region.
2. Use **Azure Load Balancer** or **Application Gateway** with health probes.
3. Store web content in **Zone-redundant Storage (ZRS)** for durability.
4. Set up **Auto-Scale rules** on the VMSS or App Service Plan.
5. Monitor availability via **Azure Monitor alerts.**

Best Practice:

- Always combine **availability sets/zones** with auto-scaling and load balancing.
- Review SLA documentation to align design with business expectations.
- Test failover and autoscaling scenarios periodically.

Scenario 3: Implementing Backup and Recovery for VMs

CHALLENGE: A critical SQL VM must be backed up daily, with 30-day retention and support for file-level restore.

Approach:

1. Create a **Recovery Services Vault** in the same region as the VM.

2. Enable backup with the following settings:

   - Daily backup at 2 AM
   - Retention for 30 days
   - Soft delete enabled

3. Configure file-level restore via the Portal as needed.

4. Monitor backup success with **Azure Monitor logs**.

Best Practice:

- Use **tags** to identify backup policies (Backup: DailySQL).
- Automate backup enablement via policy for new VMs.
- Conduct **quarterly restore drills**.

Scenario 4: Troubleshooting a VM Connectivity Issue

CHALLENGE: A production VM is unreachable over RDP and its web app is timing out.

Approach:

1. Use **Azure Network Watcher**:
   - IP flow verify: confirm NSG rule status
   - Effective security rules: confirm port 3389 and 443/80 access
2. Verify **route table and DNS** settings.
3. Check if the public IP is dynamic and has changed.
4. Review recent **Azure Activity Logs** for NSG or UDR changes.

Best Practice:

- Always **associate NSGs at subnet and NIC level** for clarity.

- Enable **just-in-time VM access** for admin ports to reduce exposure.
- Use **alerts** on NSG rule changes and VM shutdowns.

Scenario 5: Managing Costs in a Multi-Team Environment

CHALLENGE: Your organization has dev, test, and production environments. Teams often forget to delete unused resources.

Approach:

1. Apply **tags** to all resources: Environment, Owner, Project.
2. Create **Azure Budgets** per environment and owner.
3. Schedule a weekly **Azure Automation Runbook** to:
   - Identify untagged resources
   - Shutdown non-prod VMs after hours
   - Email reminders for orphaned resources
4. Use **Azure Policy** to enforce tagging and restrict expensive SKUs.

Best Practice:

- Tagging should be part of every IaC deployment pipeline.
- Define lifecycle policies for non-prod resources.

- Use **Cost Analysis** to educate teams on their monthly usage.

Scenario 6: Scaling a Stateless API with VMSS

CHALLENGE: A containerized API deployed on VMs needs to auto-scale with traffic while maintaining zero downtime during updates.

Approach:

1. Use **Virtual Machine Scale Sets (VMSS)** with custom images or ARM templates.
2. Enable **autoscale rules** based on CPU or queue length.
3. Deploy updates using **Rolling Upgrade policy**.
4. Use **Azure Load Balancer** with health probes to manage routing.

Best Practice:

- Set scale-in and scale-out thresholds with a buffer to prevent oscillation.
- Ensure logging and monitoring is consistent across instances.
- Use **Azure DevOps Pipelines or GitHub Actions** for blue/green deployment.

Scenario 7: Auditing and Compliance Reporting

CHALLENGE: Your organization requires monthly compliance reports showing user activity, resource creation, and access changes.

Approach:

1. Enable **Azure Activity Logs** and forward to **Log Analytics.**

2. Use **KQL** queries to extract relevant data:

   ○ VM creation/deletion

   ○ Role assignments

   ○ Firewall or NSG changes

3. Build a **workbook dashboard** with compliance KPIs.

4. Export results to CSV and email to stakeholders.

Best Practice:

- Automate report generation via Logic Apps or Function Apps.
- Store logs in centralized **Log Analytics Workspace** with 1-year retention.
- Monitor for policy violations with **Azure Security Center.**

Scenario 8: Securing App Secrets with Azure Key Vault

CHALLENGE: A .NET web app stores credentials in configuration files.

Approach:

1. Deploy an **Azure Key Vault** in the same region.
2. Grant the app's managed identity Key Vault Secrets User role.
3. Update the app config to reference Key Vault URIs.
4. Enable logging for secret access and failed attempts.

Best Practice:

- Use **access policies** or RBAC depending on vault type.
- Rotate secrets periodically and automate expiration notifications.
- Enable **purge protection and soft delete**.

Scenario 9: Responding to Performance Degradation

CHALLENGE: Users report that the application is slow during peak hours.

Approach:

1. Use **Azure Monitor** and **Application Insights** to review:

○ Response times

○ Failed requests

○ Backend dependency calls

2. Scale app infrastructure based on metrics:

○ VMSS: scale-out based on CPU

- App Service Plan: scale based on HTTP queue length

3. Use **Log Analytics** to correlate issues with configuration changes or high loads.

Best Practice:

- Configure **autoscale rules** that anticipate demand (e.g., based on historical patterns).
- Use **distributed tracing** with Application Insights.
- Document all mitigations for future audits.

Summary Best Practices by Domain

Domain	Best Practices
Identity & Access	Use least privilege RBAC, role assignment at lowest scope
Compute	Use availability sets/zones and VMSS; automate backup and monitoring
Networking	Document NSGs and UDRs; enable JIT and diagnostics
Storage	Use proper redundancy; automate tiering; enforce encryption
Monitoring	Centralize logging; standardize alerts; automate remediation with runbooks
Cost Management	Apply tags; set budgets; automate shutdown of idle resources
Automation	Use Functions, Logic Apps, and Policies for governance
Security	Store secrets in Key Vault; enable logging and soft delete

Final Thought

TO EXCEL BEYOND CERTIFICATION, Azure Administrators must bridge theory and practice. Certification validates your baseline knowledge—but daily success hinges on implementing efficient, secure, cost-effective, and compliant architectures. Mastering real-world scenarios and embedding best practices into every deployment will position you as not just an Azure Administrator, but a trusted cloud leader.

Career Pathways and Specializations

AFTER ACHIEVING THE AZ-104 Microsoft Azure Administrator certification, many professionals find themselves asking: "What's next?" The AZ-104 validates core administrative skills and understanding of Azure's foundational services, but it's only the beginning of a much broader journey. Whether your goals are focused on deepening technical expertise, leading cloud architecture initiatives, advancing into security or DevOps, or moving into management roles, the cloud ecosystem offers diverse and dynamic pathways.

This section explores potential career directions available to Azure-certified professionals. We'll break down the most prominent specializations, certifications that align with each, typical job roles, required skill sets, and strategies for continuous growth. You'll also learn how to align your interests and strengths with industry demand to plan a fulfilling, long-term cloud career.

Why Specialize?

THE BREADTH OF THE cloud landscape makes it impossible to master everything. Specialization allows you to:

- **Develop deep expertise** in a domain (e.g., security, networking, DevOps)
- **Target higher-paying and higher-impact roles**
- **Align your skills with organizational priorities**
- **Become a go-to expert within your team or industry**

By specializing, you transform from a generalist into a domain leader—critical for career advancement and job security in a competitive field.

Career Path 1: Cloud Security Engineer

OVERVIEW: Focus on protecting cloud environments from threats, enforcing compliance, and implementing identity and access controls.

Key Responsibilities:

- Configure security controls across Azure resources
- Manage identity, MFA, and conditional access
- Monitor and respond to security threats using Azure Defender and Sentinel
- Enforce governance through Azure Policy and Blueprints

Recommended Certifications:

- **AZ-500**: Microsoft Azure Security Technologies
- **SC-200**: Microsoft Security Operations Analyst
- **SC-300**: Identity and Access Administrator

Daily Tools:

- Microsoft Defender for Cloud
- Microsoft Sentinel

- Azure Key Vault
- Azure AD Identity Protection

Example Role Titles:

- Cloud Security Engineer
- Security Operations Analyst (SecOps)
- Identity & Access Management Engineer

Career Path 2: Azure DevOps Engineer

OVERVIEW: Combine software development and IT operations to streamline the lifecycle of applications and infrastructure.

Key Responsibilities:

- Automate deployments with CI/CD pipelines
- Use Infrastructure as Code (IaC) with ARM/Bicep or Terraform
- Monitor releases and application performance
- Collaborate across development and operations teams

Recommended Certifications:

- **AZ-400**: Azure DevOps Engineer Expert
- **GitHub Actions** & **Azure DevOps Services** mastery
- Optional: Terraform Associate (HashiCorp)

Daily Tools:

- Azure DevOps
- GitHub Actions
- Terraform or Bicep
- Application Insights
- Azure Monitor

Example Role Titles:

- DevOps Engineer
- Site Reliability Engineer (SRE)
- Cloud Platform Engineer

Career Path 3: Azure Solutions Architect

OVERVIEW: Design end-to-end Azure solutions for applications, data, networking, and security with scalability and resilience in mind.

Key Responsibilities:

- Define architecture for enterprise apps and services
- Select the right Azure services for performance, availability, and cost
- Lead migration and modernization initiatives

- Create high-level diagrams, documentation, and governance models

Recommended Certifications:

- **AZ-305**: Azure Solutions Architect Expert
- **TOGAF**, **Well-Architected Framework**, or other architectural methodologies

Daily Tools:

- Azure Architecture Center
- Azure Migrate
- ARM templates / Terraform
- API Management

Example Role Titles:

- Cloud Solutions Architect
- Enterprise Architect
- Lead Azure Consultant

Career Path 4: Data Engineer / AI Engineer

OVERVIEW: Focus on designing data pipelines, integrating storage and analytics tools, and enabling AI-driven insights.

Key Responsibilities:

- Build and maintain data pipelines (ETL/ELT)
- Manage data lakes, Azure Synapse, and SQL Databases
- Implement ML/AI solutions using Azure Cognitive Services and ML Studio
- Ensure compliance and data governance

Recommended Certifications:

- **DP-203**: Data Engineering on Microsoft Azure
- **AI-102**: Designing and Implementing an Azure AI Solution
- **DP-100**: Azure Data Scientist Associate (optional)

Daily Tools:

- Azure Synapse Analytics
- Azure Data Factory
- Azure Data Lake
- Azure Machine Learning

Example Role Titles:

- Data Engineer
- Machine Learning Engineer
- AI Solution Developer

Career Path 5: Cloud Infrastructure Engineer / Architect

OVERVIEW: Focus on architecting, automating, and scaling infrastructure in Azure, including networking, compute, and storage.

Key Responsibilities:

- Implement hybrid networks, VNet peering, ExpressRoute
- Manage high availability and DR strategies
- Automate VM, container, and serverless deployments
- Tune infrastructure for performance and cost

Recommended Certifications:

- **AZ-700**: Designing and Implementing Azure Networking Solutions
- **AZ-305**: Solutions Architect Expert
- Kubernetes certifications (CKA, AKS) for container focus

Daily Tools:

- Azure CLI / PowerShell
- Azure Load Balancer, Application Gateway
- Network Watcher

- Azure Automation

Example Role Titles:

- Cloud Infrastructure Engineer
- Azure Networking Specialist
- Azure Platform Architect

Career Path 6: Technical Leadership / Management

OVERVIEW: Transition from hands-on roles into leadership, overseeing teams, budgets, architecture decisions, and strategic initiatives.

Key Responsibilities:

- Manage teams of cloud engineers or architects
- Align cloud strategy with business goals
- Handle vendor negotiations and cost governance
- Oversee security, compliance, and cross-team collaboration

Certifications:

- Focus less on technical, more on business acumen
- **ITIL 4**, **PMI-PMP**, **Microsoft Certified: Cloud Fundamentals**
- MBA or leadership-focused certifications (optional)

Example Role Titles:

- Cloud Practice Lead
- Cloud Engineering Manager
- Director of Cloud Infrastructure

Strategic Steps to Advance

1. **Assess your interests and work strengths**
   - Love scripting? Consider DevOps.
   - Enjoy visualizing systems? Architect.
   - Passionate about security? Go for AZ-500 and SC-200.
2. **Learn continuously**
   - Subscribe to Azure blogs, GitHub repos, newsletters.
   - Attend MS Ignite, virtual events, user groups.
3. **Document your projects**
   - Use GitHub for code samples, Bicep/Terraform templates.
   - Create a technical blog or internal wiki contributions.
4. **Network and mentor**
   - Join Azure-focused LinkedIn or Discord communities.

○ Mentor junior admins or conduct internal training.

5. **Get practical exposure**

○ Volunteer for initiatives like cost optimization or zero trust architecture in your current role.

Summary of Specializations

Specialization	Key Certification(s)	Role Focus
Security	AZ-500, SC-200, SC-300	Protect resources, monitor threats
DevOps	AZ-400, Terraform Associate	Automate, deploy, and monitor systems
Architect	AZ-305	Design enterprise cloud environments
Data / AI	DP-203, AI-102	Work with data pipelines and ML models
Infrastructure	AZ-700, AZ-305	Build robust compute and network layers
Leadership	N/A or ITIL, PMP	Team, strategy, and cross-functional ops

Final Thought

THE CLOUD IS EVOLVING fast, and so should you. Whether you're drawn to automation, data, security, or big-picture design, the AZ-104 certification opens doors—but it's up to you to walk through the one that matches your aspirations. By pursuing specialization, aligning with business value, and committing to continuous improvement, you'll not only stand out—you'll lead.

Continuous Learning in the Azure Ecosystem

STAYING RELEVANT AS a cloud professional requires more than certification—it demands a commitment to continuous learning. Azure evolves rapidly, with new services, deprecations, updated best practices, and shifting priorities. As an Azure Administrator or cloud specialist, continuous learning isn't just beneficial—it's essential for long-term career growth, service reliability, and innovation.

This section provides a deep dive into how to adopt and sustain a continuous learning mindset. It explores structured and unstructured learning strategies, key tools and platforms for staying updated, and ways to integrate learning into your daily workflow without burnout. Whether you're aiming for your next certification, leading innovation in your team, or simply keeping your knowledge fresh, this chapter will help you build a lifelong learning system within the dynamic Azure ecosystem.

Why Continuous Learning Matters

- **Cloud services change weekly**: What was true three months ago may now be deprecated or modified.
- **Business needs evolve**: Today's solution may not be tomorrow's priority.
- **Security and compliance expectations increase**: New regulations, zero-trust models, and threat vectors demand current knowledge.
- **Automation is increasing**: Staying ahead means embracing DevOps, IaC, and scripting fluency.

- **Competitive advantage**: Employers and clients seek professionals who stay ahead of the curve.

Microsoft's Learning Ecosystem

1. Microsoft Learn

MICROSOFT LEARN IS the official and free learning platform provided by Microsoft. It features:

- Role-based learning paths
- Interactive modules with sandbox environments
- Exam preparation paths for certifications
- Hands-on labs and exercises
- Integration with GitHub repositories and sample code

Popular learning paths for ongoing development:

- *Manage identities and governance in Azure*
- *Implement and manage storage in Azure*
- *Automate infrastructure using ARM and Bicep*
- *Administer containers using AKS*
- *Implement security and compliance in Azure*

Use CLI to bookmark or track progress:

az extension add—name learn

az learn progress—path "Implement Security with Azure Defender"

---

2. Certification Roadmaps

STAYING CERTIFIED IS one of the clearest ways to demonstrate continued learning. Microsoft's certification path includes:

- **Fundamentals (e.g., AZ-900, AI-900, SC-900)**
- **Associate (e.g., AZ-104, DP-203, SC-200)**
- **Expert (e.g., AZ-305, AZ-400)**
- **Specialty (e.g., SAP, IoT, Cosmos DB)**

Recertification now involves completing Microsoft Learn renewals, which are free and must be done annually for most associate and expert credentials.

Track upcoming renewals at:https://learn.microsoft.com/en-us/certifications/renew-your-certification/

Integrating Learning into Your Workflow

1. Daily Reading and Watching

- **Azure Updates Feed**:https://azure.microsoft.com/en-us/updates/
- **Tech Community Blog**:https://techcommunity.microsoft.com[7]
- **YouTube Channels:**

---

7. https://techcommunity.microsoft.com/

  - ○ Microsoft Azure
  - ○ John Savill's Technical Training
  - ○ Learn with Sentdex (for Python + Azure integrations)
- **Newsletters**:
  - ○ Azure Weekly
  - ○ Azure DevOps Weekly
  - ○ Morning Brew (for general cloud/dev news)

USE RSS READERS LIKE Feedly to consolidate and filter new Azure announcements.

2. GitHub and Labs

- Join active repositories:
  - ○ Azure Quickstart Templates[8]
  - ○ Azure Samples[9]
  - ○ Awesome Azure[10]

EXPLORE AND FORK IAC templates, scripts, and Bicep modules to test new features.

---

8. https://github.com/Azure/azure-quickstart-templates
9. https://github.com/Azure-Samples
10. https://github.com/rosshamish/Awesome-Azure

3. Personal Lab Environment

SET UP A SANDBOX FOR experimentation:

- Use a **free-tier Azure subscription** or allocate a training budget
- Automate environment creation with Bicep or Terraform
- Schedule weekly "lab hours" to try:
  - New storage types
  - Custom policies
  - Zero-trust configurations
  - Azure OpenAI integration

Example script to deploy a Bicep-based VNet for testing:

```
az deployment group create \
—resource-group MyLabRG \
—template-file ./vnet.bicep \
—parameters environment=dev location=uksouth
```

Community and Peer-Based Learning

1. Join Professional Communities

- **Microsoft Tech Community**

- **Reddit**: r/AZURE, r/devops, r/cloudcomputing
- **LinkedIn groups**: Azure-focused or general cloud
- **Discord and Slack**: Cloud-specific servers
- **Local and virtual user groups**: Meetup.com often hosts Azure events

2. Attend Conferences and Webinars

- **Microsoft Ignite**
- **Azure OpenDev**
- **CloudSkills.io Live**
- **Pluralsight LIVE**
- **DevOpsDays and Kubernetes conferences**

THESE EVENTS OFTEN provide labs, career panels, and real-world demos.

3. Teach Others

TEACHING IS A HIGH-impact way to solidify your own understanding:

- Write blog posts or LinkedIn articles
- Host lunch-and-learns or webinars
- Answer questions on Stack Overflow or Microsoft Q&A

- Contribute to open-source Azure projects or documentation

Tools for Managing Your Learning Journey

Tool	Purpose	Example Use Case
Notion/ Obsidian	Track learning goals and certifications	Create a "learning dashboard" for weekly progress
Trello/ Asana	Task-based tracking of study goals	Kanban board for certification topics
Anki/ RemNote	Flashcards with spaced repetition	Memorizing CLI syntax or Azure service tiers
GitHub	Version control and code sharing	Store scripts, templates, and practice labs
Azure DevOps	Document and version your lab pipelines	Practice CI/CD pipelines for learning exercises

Avoiding Burnout While Learning

- **Pace yourself**: Not every update needs deep analysis. Focus on relevance.

- **Use cycles**: 30-day focused sprints with a goal (e.g., learn Bicep, prep for AZ-305).

- **Alternate learning formats**: Mix labs, reading, watching, and doing.

- **Celebrate milestones**: Track achievements, even small ones like completing a module.

- **Schedule breaks**: Take weekly off-days from learning to prevent fatigue.

Monthly Learning Plan Template

WEEK 1:

- Complete 1 Microsoft Learn module (e.g., Azure Monitor)
- Read Azure Updates for past 2 weeks
- Join 1 webinar or Meetup

Week 2:

- Deploy a hands-on lab (e.g., Azure Policy + RBAC combination)
- Summarize learnings in your notes or blog
- Watch a deep dive video

Week 3:

- Take a mini-practice test (10–15 questions)
- Review Azure Advisor recommendations in your environment
- Attend a tech community discussion

Week 4:

- Try out a new Bicep or Terraform deployment
- Share your progress on LinkedIn

- Plan next month's goal (e.g., prepare for AZ-500)

Summary

CONTINUOUS LEARNING in Azure is not a luxury—it's a professional necessity. As the platform evolves, your ability to keep pace with changes determines your credibility, impact, and career trajectory. By building structured learning habits, engaging with the community, and dedicating time to experimentation, you ensure not just survival but sustained excellence in a world powered by cloud innovation. Let learning be your competitive edge, your career engine, and your path to mastery.

Building a Professional Portfolio

IN THE RAPIDLY EVOLVING landscape of cloud technology, practical experience and demonstrable skill often speak louder than credentials alone. A well-crafted professional portfolio allows Azure administrators and cloud practitioners to showcase real-world competencies, projects, and problem-solving abilities in ways that a resume or certification badge cannot. As organizations increasingly look for evidence of hands-on ability and innovation, a portfolio becomes your strongest advocate—proving not just that you know, but that you can do.

This section will guide you through designing, creating, and evolving a professional Azure portfolio. It covers the types of projects to include, how to document them, which platforms to use, and strategies for maximizing visibility and impact. Whether you're job hunting, freelancing, consulting, or aiming for internal promotion, your portfolio will help set you apart in the cloud workforce.

Why Build a Portfolio?

- **Demonstrates applied knowledge**: Showcases how you solve real problems using Azure services.

- **Validates hands-on experience**: Especially important if you're transitioning roles or industries.

- **Improves job prospects**: Helps hiring managers and recruiters see your capabilities quickly.

- **Supports internal advancement**: Provides evidence for performance reviews and promotions.

- **Builds personal confidence**: Reinforces your skills and provides a reference base for future work.

Core Components of a Cloud Portfolio

YOUR AZURE PORTFOLIO should be structured to highlight both breadth and depth of experience. The key components include:

1. **Profile and Bio**

   ○ Who you are, your current role, and cloud goals.

   ○ Summary of certifications and technical interests.

2. **Project Repository**

   ○ Hands-on Azure projects with source code, diagrams, and documentation.

○ Can include ARM/Bicep templates, PowerShell scripts, Terraform modules, and YAML pipelines.

3. **Case Studies**

○ Real or simulated business problems you've solved.

○ Clear before-and-after state, architecture decisions, and outcomes.

4. **Certifications and Learning**

○ Badges from Microsoft Learn and certification credentials.

○ Reflection posts about what you learned from each course or exam.

5. **Technical Blog or Documentation**

○ Guides, tutorials, or write-ups of how you built your projects.

○ Explanation of best practices, failures, and lessons learned.

6. **Contribution History**

○ GitHub pull requests, issues, or open-source contributions.

○ Stack Overflow answers, community articles, or Microsoft Tech Community posts.

Suggested Project Ideas for AZ-104-Level Portfolios

THESE PROJECTS VALIDATE your understanding of core AZ-104 skills:

1. RBAC & Azure AD Identity Management

- Deploy a sample web app secured with Azure AD.
- Implement RBAC for developers, auditors, and operators.
- Document access decisions and audit logs.

2. Virtual Network and Security Configuration

- Set up a hub-and-spoke network topology.
- Implement NSGs, route tables, and a firewall.
- Validate traffic flow using Azure Network Watcher.

3. IaaS Compute and Backup

- Deploy an autoscaling VMSS with custom scripts and monitoring.
- Configure backup using Recovery Services Vault.
- Demonstrate file-level restore from backup.

4. Storage Lifecycle and Access Control

- Create a storage account with multiple blob tiers.

- Automate tier transitions and logging.
- Implement SAS tokens and Azure AD-based access.

5. Monitoring and Alert Automation

- Set up Azure Monitor metrics, diagnostic logs, and alerts.
- Create an action group with webhook and Logic App integration.
- Document a simulated incident response.

6. Infrastructure as Code

- Deploy a full environment using Bicep or Terraform:
  - VM + VNet + NSG + storage
- Include parameterization, tagging, and output validation.

Tools to Host and Present Your Portfolio

Platform	Purpose	Notes
GitHub	Code, scripts, documentation, automation	Add README.md, LICENSE, and screenshots
LinkedIn	Highlight certifications and link projects	Use featured section for top projects
Dev.to / Medium	Blog-style writeups and tutorials	Drive traffic and engagement
GitHub Pages	Free personal website with portfolio layout	Customize with Jekyll or static site builder
Notion	Integrated wiki-like portfolio space	Combine resume, projects, and learning logs

INCLUDE README TEMPLATES like:

Azure VMSS Auto-Scaling Deployment

Overview

This project demonstrates how to deploy an Azure VM Scale Set with autoscaling and diagnostic monitoring using Bicep.

Architecture

- Azure Load Balancer (standard)

- VMSS with Ubuntu 20.04

- Log Analytics workspace

- Alert rule on CPU threshold

Deployment

```bash
az deployment group create \
—resource-group myRG \
—template-file ./vmss.bicep
```

Lessons Learned

- Scaling rules must be tuned carefully to avoid flapping.
- Diagnostic settings must be enabled at creation for consistent data.

PROJECT DOCUMENTATION and Visuals

Every project should include:

- **Architecture diagram** (draw.io, Lucidchart, Visio)
- **README file** with purpose, setup instructions, and outcomes
- **Code snippets** or full templates/scripts
- **Screenshots** of deployments, logs, and validation steps
- **Reflections** on challenges, decisions, and what could be improved

---

PORTFOLIO GROWTH STRATEGY

1. **Start small**: Choose one domain and deploy a real-world example.

2. **Build consistency**: Add new projects monthly or quarterly.

3. **Iterate**: Refactor older projects with new skills (e.g., migrate from ARM to Bicep).

4. **Version your work**: Use Git tags or branches for portfolio milestones.

5. **Use metrics**: Track GitHub stars, site traffic, or engagement.

6. **Cross-link content**: Embed links in resumes, blogs, and LinkedIn.

SHOWCASING YOUR PORTFOLIO

- **In job applications**: Link directly to your GitHub or portfolio page.

- **In interviews**: Walk through a specific project live or via slides.

- **During performance reviews**: Demonstrate contributions and growth.

- **On social media**: Share learning, labs, and completed modules publicly.

BEST PRACTICES FOR a Strong Portfolio

- **Quality over quantity**: 5 strong, well-documented projects > 20 unfinished ones.

- **Focus on impact**: Highlight what problem was solved, not just what was built.

- **Keep it updated**: Show that you're active and committed to growth.

- **Use clean structure**: Consistent folders, naming, and markdown formatting.

- **Document failures too**: Employers value your ability to learn from mistakes.

SUMMARY

Your professional portfolio is more than a collection of projects—it's a dynamic reflection of your capabilities, mindset, and growth. It tells a story of not just what you've done, but how you approach problems and adapt to new technologies. By investing time in building and maintaining a well-organized, insightful portfolio, you stand out in the increasingly crowded field of cloud professionals. It's not just about proving your skills—it's about showing the world what you're capable of delivering in Azure.

Chapter 9: Appendices

Glossary of Terms

UNDERSTANDING CLOUD terminology is essential to mastering the Microsoft Azure ecosystem, especially when preparing for certifications like the AZ-104. This glossary provides clear, concise definitions of the most important Azure-specific terms, acronyms, and technical concepts covered in the exam. Use this reference to reinforce your understanding of key ideas and clarify any ambiguous terms encountered during study, practice, or hands-on work in Azure.

A

ACCESS CONTROL (IAM)

Azure's Identity and Access Management feature, allowing users to assign roles to manage access to resources. It supports Role-Based Access Control (RBAC) to enforce least-privilege access.

Active Directory (Azure AD)

Microsoft's multi-tenant cloud-based directory and identity management service. Provides SSO, conditional access, MFA, and device registration capabilities.

AKS (Azure Kubernetes Service)

A managed container orchestration service using Kubernetes, allowing for automated deployment, scaling, and management of containerized applications.

ARM (Azure Resource Manager)

The deployment and management service for Azure. All resource deployments use ARM templates or APIs. ARM ensures consistent resource provisioning and enables tagging, access control, and auditing.

Availability Set

A logical grouping of VMs that allows Azure to distribute them across multiple physical hardware to reduce downtime from hardware failure or maintenance.

Availability Zone

Physically separate datacenter locations within an Azure region, offering high availability and fault tolerance for applications and data.

B

BICEP

A domain-specific language (DSL) for deploying Azure resources declaratively. Simplifies authoring of ARM templates.

Blob Storage

Azure's object storage solution for unstructured data. Supports tiered access (Hot, Cool, Archive) and integrates with SAS tokens and lifecycle policies.

Backup Vault

Also known as Recovery Services Vault, it stores backup data for Azure VMs, files, and workloads. Enables long-term retention and granular restores.

Budget (Azure Cost Management)

Tool to set spending limits and trigger notifications when resource consumption exceeds thresholds.

C

CLOUD SHELL

An online Bash and PowerShell terminal accessible via Azure Portal. Pre-configured with common tools like Azure CLI, Git, and Terraform.

CLI (Command-Line Interface)

Azure CLI is a cross-platform command-line tool for managing Azure resources. Can be run from local terminal, Cloud Shell, or scripts.

Conditional Access

A feature of Azure AD that enforces policies based on user, device, location, and risk conditions to grant or deny access.

Content Delivery Network (CDN)

Delivers static content from geographically distributed servers to reduce latency and improve load times.

Custom Role

A user-defined RBAC role tailored to specific permission requirements not met by built-in roles.

D

DATA LAKE

Highly scalable storage repository that supports big data analytics. Azure Data Lake Storage Gen2 combines capabilities of Blob storage and Hadoop-compatible access.

DNS Zone

Represents a domain namespace and manages DNS records like A, CNAME, and MX. Azure DNS is used to host and resolve these zones.

Disk Encryption (ADE)

Azure Disk Encryption uses BitLocker (Windows) or DM-Crypt (Linux) to encrypt OS and data disks at rest.

Diagnostics Settings

Configuration that routes platform metrics and logs to Log Analytics, Event Hubs, or Storage Accounts for auditing and analysis.

E

EXPRESSROUTE

Provides dedicated, private connectivity between an on-premises network and Azure, bypassing the public internet for enhanced security and performance.

Elasticity

The ability of cloud resources to dynamically scale in or out to match workload demands. Typically implemented with autoscale rules.

Endpoint Protection

Security services that monitor and protect cloud resources, like Azure Defender and Microsoft Sentinel.

F

FAILOVER

Switching to a standby resource or region when a primary system fails. Azure services such as Traffic Manager and Geo-redundant Storage support automated failover.

Firewall (Azure Firewall)

A managed, stateful network security service to control inbound and outbound traffic across Azure VNets and subscriptions.

Function App

Azure's serverless compute service where code executes in response to events (e.g., HTTP requests, timers, message queues).

G

GEO-REDUNDANT STORAGE (GRS)

A replication option that copies data to a paired region to provide disaster recovery capabilities.

Governance

The set of policies, role assignments, and compliance mechanisms that enforce security, operational, and financial boundaries in Azure.

Guided Lab

Hands-on, interactive environment (usually from Microsoft Learn) for practicing tasks in a controlled sandbox.

H

HIGH AVAILABILITY (HA)

Architecture design that ensures service continuity and minimal downtime through redundancy, zoning, and failover mechanisms.

Hybrid Identity

An integration of on-premises Active Directory with Azure AD using Azure AD Connect for unified identity and access management.

I

INFRASTRUCTURE AS CODE (IaC)

The practice of managing and provisioning infrastructure using code (e.g., ARM, Bicep, Terraform) for repeatability and automation.

Initiative (Azure Policy)

A collection of policy definitions grouped to enforce specific compliance goals. Helps manage large-scale governance rules.

Identity Protection

Azure AD capability that uses machine learning to detect and respond to risky sign-ins and compromised users.

J

JUST-IN-TIME (JIT) VM Access

Security mechanism to limit exposure of management ports by enabling temporary access on-demand.

K

KEY VAULT

Securely stores and manages sensitive information like secrets, keys, and certificates. Integrates with managed identities and RBAC.

L

LOAD BALANCER

Distributes inbound traffic across multiple Azure resources to ensure high availability and performance. Comes in Basic and Standard SKUs.

Lifecycle Management

Blob storage feature that automates transition of blobs between access tiers or deletion after a set retention period.

Log Analytics

Query tool for analyzing logs collected in Azure Monitor. Uses Kusto Query Language (KQL) for powerful filtering and visualization.

M

MANAGED IDENTITY

Automatically managed identity used to authenticate with Azure services without managing credentials.

Metric Alerts

Notifications triggered by performance thresholds (e.g., CPU > 80%) to inform or automate responses.

Marketplace

Azure's digital storefront for third-party applications, virtual machines, and managed solutions.

N

NETWORK SECURITY GROUP (NSG)

Controls inbound and outbound traffic at the subnet or NIC level. Uses rules based on source/destination IP, protocol, and port.

NSG Rule Priority

Numerical value (100–4096) that determines rule processing order; lower numbers are evaluated first.

O

OPERATIONAL EXCELLENCE

One of the Azure Well-Architected Framework pillars focusing on monitoring, automation, and recoverability.

P

PRIVATE ENDPOINT

A network interface that connects you privately and securely to a service powered by Azure Private Link.

Public IP

Externally accessible address assigned to Azure resources like VMs or Load Balancers.

Policy Effect

The action a policy takes when a resource is evaluated: audit, deny, append, deployIfNotExists, etc.

Q

QUOTA

Soft limits set on Azure resources to prevent over-consumption. Can be increased via support requests.

R

RESOURCE GROUP

A logical container that holds related Azure resources for management and billing purposes.

RBAC (Role-Based Access Control)

Authorization system based on roles assigned to users, groups, or service principals scoped to Azure resources.

Recovery Point

A saved state of data or configuration used to restore Azure VMs or files in backup scenarios.

S

STORAGE ACCOUNT

A container for blobs, files, queues, and tables. Controls access, performance tier, redundancy, and networking.

Service Principal

A security identity used by apps and automation tools to access Azure resources securely.

Soft Delete

Feature that retains deleted data (e.g., blobs, Key Vault secrets, backups) for a specified period to allow recovery.

T

TAG

Key-value pair assigned to resources for categorization, cost management, and automation. E.g., Environment=Production.

Terraform

Open-source Infrastructure as Code tool by HashiCorp that allows declarative Azure deployments.

U

UPDATE DOMAIN

Logical grouping in Availability Sets to ensure VMs are not updated simultaneously during maintenance.

V

VIRTUAL NETWORK (VNET)

A private, isolated network in Azure. Supports IP addressing, DNS, routing, NSGs, and peering.

VNet Peering

Links VNets for internal connectivity without gateways. Supports both same and cross-region peering.

VM Scale Set (VMSS)

Manages a group of identical, load-balanced VMs that can automatically scale based on demand.

W

WEB APP (APP SERVICE)

Azure's PaaS offering for hosting websites, REST APIs, and mobile backends. Supports scaling, CI/CD, and custom domains.

Workspace (Log Analytics)

Logical container for log data from Azure Monitor, used for centralized querying and analysis.

Z

ZONE-REDUNDANT STORAGE (ZRS)

Stores data redundantly across availability zones to ensure resiliency against datacenter-level failures.

Symbols

$RESOURCEID

Generic placeholder used in scripts and commands to reference the full Azure Resource Manager ID of an object.

az

Azure CLI command prefix. Used to manage and automate Azure resources through shell scripting.

Summary

THIS GLOSSARY IS YOUR quick-access reference for AZ-104 and beyond. Understanding these terms and how they interrelate is foundational to working efficiently with Azure services. Refer to this list throughout your study and practice to reinforce comprehension and clarify uncertainties as you navigate through increasingly complex Azure scenarios.

Resources for Further Learning

MASTERING MICROSOFT Azure and achieving the AZ-104 certification is only the beginning of your journey. The cloud evolves rapidly—new features are added weekly, and best practices shift as services mature. To remain a competent and valuable Azure Administrator, you must continue to grow your skills through structured learning, active engagement with the community, and hands-on experimentation.

This section presents a curated, in-depth guide to the best resources for advancing your Azure knowledge beyond this book. These include Microsoft official materials, third-party learning platforms, books, newsletters, videos, hands-on labs, and community events. Each resource is categorized with use cases, recommended audiences, and practical tips for integration into your ongoing learning path.

Microsoft Official Learning Platforms

Microsoft Learn

HTTPS://LEARN.MICROSOFT.com/training/[11]

Microsoft Learn is the primary source of free, up-to-date, role-based Azure training. Content is segmented by roles, products, and certifications.

Best For:

- Structured, interactive modules
- Certification exam preparation
- Sandbox environments with no Azure subscription required

Key Paths:

- *Azure Administrator (AZ-104)*
- *Implementing Azure Governance*
- *Monitoring and Backing Up Azure Resources*

Tip: Create a free Microsoft Learn account to track progress and earn trophies and achievements.

Microsoft Certifications Dashboard

HTTPS://LEARN.MICROSOFT.com/en-us/certifications[12]

---

11. https://learn.microsoft.com/training/

12. https://learn.microsoft.com/en-us/certifications

This portal provides certification paths, skill outlines, renewal information, and exam scheduling.

Use It To:

- Track your active certifications
- Register for exams via Pearson VUE
- Renew credentials by passing free assessments

Microsoft Tech Community

HTTPS://TECHCOMMUNITY.microsoft.com[13]

The Tech Community provides blogs, forums, events, and discussions across Microsoft's cloud and enterprise stack.

Recommended Areas:

- Azure Blog (announcements and roadmaps)
- Azure Governance & Management
- Security, Networking, Identity, and Compliance communities

---

13. https://techcommunity.microsoft.com/

Books and eBooks

Microsoft Press Titles

- *Exam Ref AZ-104 Microsoft Azure Administrator* by Harshul Patel

A Microsoft-authorized, exam-focused reference covering core AZ-104 domains.

- *Inside the Microsoft Cloud* by Microsoft MVPs

Offers architectural insights for building cloud solutions at scale.

Other Recommended Titles

- *Learn Azure in a Month of Lunches* by Iain Foulds

Great for beginners; step-by-step labs for real-world deployment tasks.

- *Azure Infrastructure as Code* by Henry Been

Deep dive into deploying and managing Azure with Bicep, ARM, and Terraform.

- *The Phoenix Project* by Gene Kim

While not Azure-specific, it provides foundational thinking in DevOps and systems administration.

TIP: Use Kindle or O'Reilly Learning to access previews and read on the go.

Video-Based Learning

Microsoft Official YouTube Channels

- *Microsoft Azure*

  Tutorials, product demos, and conference content.

- *Microsoft Developer*

  Focused on building applications with Azure services.

- *Microsoft Learn TV*

  Weekly shows and live Q&A sessions on certifications and best practices.

Third-Party Platforms

- **LinkedIn Learning**

  Courses like "Azure Administration: The Big Picture" and "Learning PowerShell for Azure."

- **Pluralsight**

  Deep technical content for intermediate and advanced Azure professionals. Try:

  - *Managing Microsoft Azure Subscriptions and Resources*
  - *Implementing and Monitoring Azure Infrastructure*

- **Cloud Academy / A Cloud Guru**

Scenario-based labs and exam simulators tailored to Azure certification tracks.

- **John Savill's Technical Training** (YouTube)

One of the most trusted community-driven technical trainers for Azure.

Hands-On Labs and Simulators

Microsoft Learn Sandboxes

AZURE SANDBOXES LET you deploy and manage real resources without billing your subscription. Commonly used in Learn modules.

Tip: Each sandbox lasts for a limited time—use the resources wisely and clean up at the end.

Azure Dev/Test Subscriptions

SIGN UP FOR A PAY-AS-You-Go subscription with spending limits. Enable Cost Management to track real-world usage.

Use Cases:

- Deploying VMSS and NSGs
- Testing policy enforcement
- Experimenting with diagnostics, alerts, and backups

GitHub Lab Repositories

- *Azure Quickstart Templates* (https://github.com/Azure/azure-quickstart-templates)
- *Azure Bicep Examples* (https://github.com/Azure/bicep)
- *Terraform Azure Modules* (https://github.com/Azure/terraform-azurerm-modules)

TIP: Fork and customize templates to create a personal lab setup.

Newsletters and Blogs

Azure Weekly

HTTPS://AZUREWEEKLY.info[14]

A roundup of blog posts, news, and tools curated weekly.

Thomas Maurer's Blog

HTTPS://WWW.THOMASMAURER.ch[15]

Thomas is a Microsoft MVP and senior PM. His blog covers Azure tips, hybrid cloud, and server administration.

Azure DevOps Blog

HTTPS://DEVBLOGS.MICROSOFT.com/devops[16]

14. https://azureweekly.info/
15. https://www.thomasmaurer.ch/
16. https://devblogs.microsoft.com/devops

Includes CI/CD pipelines, IaC practices, and YAML strategies for Azure Pipelines.

Community and Networking Resources

Microsoft Learn Student Ambassadors and MVPs

ENGAGE WITH EXPERIENCED professionals who run meetups, blogs, and open-source projects. Follow them on LinkedIn, Twitter, or Tech Community.

Local Meetups

SEARCH FOR "AZURE" onhttps://www.meetup.com[17] to find virtual and in-person events in your area.

Reddit and Discord

- r/AZURE
- r/devops
- Discord: "Microsoft Azure" or "Cloud Study Network"

Conferences and Virtual Summits

- Microsoft Ignite (annual flagship conference)
- Microsoft Build (developer-focused event)
- Global Azure Bootcamp

---

17. https://www.meetup.com/

- Azure Summit Series

Practice Test Providers

Provider	Description
MeasureUp	Official Microsoft exam practice platform
Whizlabs	Practice questions with detailed explanations
Tutorials Dojo	Highly rated by the community, scenario-based
ExamTopics	Community-sourced, be cautious on accuracy

Tools for Learning Organization

Tool	Purpose	Example Use
Notion	Track learning goals and resources	Build a personal Azure learning dashboard
Anki	Flashcards for CLI commands	Memorize NSG syntax, storage tiers
Trello	Study roadmap	Visualize learning milestones
Obsidian	Local notes with markdown + graph view	Create a knowledge base of Azure topics

Monthly Learning Tracker Template

Week	Activities
Week 1	Complete 2 modules on Microsoft Learn, deploy VNet lab
Week 2	Read Azure Weekly, deploy ARM template, review 10 questions
Week 3	Watch John Savill video, try sandbox lab, attend meetup
Week 4	Write a blog post/tutorial, review missed practice questions

---

Final Tip

BOOKMARK YOUR MOST useful resources, and revisit them regularly. Consider building a "Cloud Learning Hub" in a Notion or GitHub repo, where you centralize your projects, study notes, scripts, and tools. Make continuous learning a habit—not just a goal—and you'll stay at the forefront of Azure evolution while growing your cloud career sustainably.

Sample Projects and Code Snippets

PRACTICAL EXPERIENCE is one of the strongest ways to reinforce your learning, demonstrate technical competency, and prepare for real-world Azure administration. This section contains detailed descriptions of sample projects aligned with the AZ-104 exam domains, complete with use cases, step-by-step tasks, and illustrative code snippets using Azure CLI, PowerShell, ARM, and Bicep templates.

These projects are structured to simulate production-like environments where administrators are expected to manage identity, compute, storage, networking, and monitoring effectively. Each project encourages modular development, use of infrastructure as code (IaC), governance enforcement, and cost-awareness—mirroring the demands of enterprise cloud management.

Project 1: Secure and Monitor a Virtual Machine

OBJECTIVE: Deploy a Linux virtual machine, configure security controls, enable diagnostics, and automate alerting.

Steps:

1. Create a resource group and virtual network:

az group create—name rg-az104-vm—location uksouth

az network vnet create \

—name vnet-az104 \

—resource-group rg-az104-vm \

—address-prefix 10.0.0.0/16 \

—subnet-name subnet-az104 \

—subnet-prefix 10.0.1.0/24

1. Create a network security group with restricted inbound rules:

az network nsg create—resource-group rg-az104-vm—name nsg-az104

az network nsg rule create \

—resource-group rg-az104-vm \

—nsg-name nsg-az104 \

—name AllowSSH \

—protocol Tcp \

—priority 1000 \

—destination-port-range 22 \

—access Allow \

—direction Inbound \

—source-address-prefixes <YourPublicIP>

1. Deploy a VM and associate it with the NSG:

az vm create \

—resource-group rg-az104-vm \

—name vm-secure \

—image UbuntuLTS \

—vnet-name vnet-az104 \

—subnet subnet-az104 \

—nsg nsg-az104 \

—admin-username azureuser \

—generate-ssh-keys

1. Enable boot diagnostics and monitor metrics:

az vm boot-diagnostics enable \

—resource-group rg-az104-vm \

—name vm-secure \

—storage https://<yourstorage>.blob.core.windows.net/

1. Configure alert for CPU > 70%:

az monitor metrics alert create \

—name HighCPUAlert \

—resource-group rg-az104-vm \

—scopes /subscriptions/<sub-id>/resourceGroups/rg-az104-vm/providers/Microsoft.Compute/virtualMachines/vm-secure \

—condition "avg Percentage CPU > 70" \

—description "CPU usage is above threshold"

Project 2: Configure Storage with Lifecycle and Access Policies

OBJECTIVE: Deploy a storage account with secure access, define lifecycle rules, and test file uploads.

Steps:

1. Create a storage account with HTTPS-only access:

az storage account create \

—name az104securestorage \

—resource-group rg-az104-vm \

—sku Standard_GRS \

—encryption-services blob \

—https-only true \

—allow-blob-public-access false

1. Create a container and upload a sample blob:

az storage container create \

—name secure-container \

—account-name az104securestorage \

—public-access off

az storage blob upload \

—container-name secure-container \

—file sample.txt \

—name sample.txt \

—account-name az104securestorage

1. Add lifecycle management rules:

{

"rules": [

{

"enabled": true,

"name": "moveToCoolTier",

```
"type": "Lifecycle",
"definition": {
"filters": {
"blobTypes": ["blockBlob"]
},
"actions": {
"baseBlob": {
"tierToCool": {
"daysAfterModificationGreaterThan": 30
},
"delete": {
"daysAfterModificationGreaterThan": 365
}
}
}
}
}
]
}
```

1. Apply the rule:

az storage account management-policy create \

—account-name az104securestorage \

—resource-group rg-az104-vm \

—policy @policy.json

Project 3: RBAC Governance and Policy Compliance

OBJECTIVE: Assign scoped access using built-in and custom roles, then enforce tagging with Azure Policy.

Steps:

1. Assign built-in Reader role to a user:

az role assignment create \

—assignee user@example.com \

—role Reader \

—scope /subscriptions/<sub-id>/resourceGroups/rg-az104-vm

1. Create a custom role with limited actions:

{

"Name": "VMStartStopOnly",

"IsCustom": true,

"Description": "Can start and stop VMs only",

"Actions": [

"Microsoft.Compute/virtualMachines/start/action",

```
"Microsoft.Compute/virtualMachines/deallocate/action"

],

"NotActions": [],

"AssignableScopes": ["/subscriptions/<sub-id>"]

}
```

1. Save and deploy:

```
az role definition create—role-definition @vmStartStopOnly.json
```

1. Enforce tagging via policy:

```
az policy definition create \

—name requireEnvironmentTag \

—display-name "Require environment tag" \

—mode All \

—rules policy-rules.json \

—params policy-params.json \

—description "Enforces the use of 'Environment' tag"
```

1. Assign the policy:

```
az policy assignment create \

—name enforceEnvironmentTag \

—policy requireEnvironmentTag \
```

```
—scope /subscriptions/<sub-id>/resourceGroups/rg-az104-vm
```

Project 4: Deploy Infrastructure with Bicep

OBJECTIVE: Build an entire environment using Bicep templates.

Bicep File: main.bicep

```
param location string = resourceGroup().location

param vmName string

param adminUsername string

resource vnet 'Microsoft.Network/virtualNetworks@2021-02-01' = {

name: 'bicep-vnet'

location: location

properties: {

addressSpace: {

addressPrefixes: ['10.0.0.0/16']

}

subnets: [

{

name: 'default'

properties: {

addressPrefix: '10.0.1.0/24'
```

```
}
}
]
}
}
resource vm 'Microsoft.Compute/virtualMachines@2021-03-01' =
{
name: vmName
location: location
properties: {
hardwareProfile: {
vmSize: 'Standard_B1s'
}
osProfile: {
computerName: vmName
adminUsername: adminUsername
adminPassword: 'YourP@ssword123'
}
storageProfile: {
imageReference: {
publisher: 'Canonical'
```

```
offer: 'UbuntuServer'
sku: '18.04-LTS'
version: 'latest'
}
osDisk: {
createOption: 'FromImage'
}
}
networkProfile: {
networkInterfaces: [
{
id: nic.id
}
]
}
}
}
resource nic 'Microsoft.Network/networkInterfaces@2021-02-01' = {
name: 'vmNic'
location: location
```

```
properties: {
ipConfigurations: [
{
name: 'ipconfig1'
properties: {
subnet: {
id: vnet.properties.subnets[0].id
}
privateIPAllocationMethod: 'Dynamic'
}
}
]
}
}
```

Deploy the template:

```
az deployment group create \
—resource-group rg-az104-vm \
—template-file main.bicep \
—parameters vmName=myVM adminUsername=azureuser
```

Project 5: Cost Management and Automation

OBJECTIVE: Set budgets, automate cost cleanup, and export usage data.

1. Create a budget:

```
az consumption budget create \
—amount 100 \
—name DevBudget \
—time-grain monthly \
—start-date 2024-01-01 \
—end-date 2024-12-31 \
—resource-group rg-az104-vm \
—notifications '{ "threshold1": { "enabled": true, "operator": "GreaterThan", "threshold": 80, "contactEmails": ["you@example.com"] } }'
```

1. Export usage to Storage:

```
az costmanagement export create \
—name MonthlyUsage \
—type Usage \
—time-frame MonthToDate \
—recurrence Monthly \
```

—storage-account-id /subscriptions/<sub-id>/resourceGroups/<rg>/providers/Microsoft.Storage/storageAccounts/<name> \

—container usage \

—file-format Csv

1. Create an Automation Account Runbook (PowerShell or Python) that deallocates non-prod VMs after hours.

Summary

THESE SAMPLE PROJECTS provide a foundation for applying AZ-104 concepts in real-world scenarios. They bridge theory and practice, helping you move from conceptual understanding to confident implementation. By saving, documenting, and iterating on these examples, you not only reinforce your learning but also build a valuable professional portfolio that showcases your administrative and automation capabilities in Azure.

API Reference Guide

APIS ARE FUNDAMENTAL to automating Azure administration, enabling integrations, enforcing policies, and managing cloud resources programmatically. For Azure Administrators, a working knowledge of how to interact with Azure services through REST APIs, the Azure CLI, PowerShell, and SDKs is essential. This section serves as a practical API reference guide, detailing key operations, common endpoints, authentication strategies, and usage patterns across core services covered in the AZ-104 exam.

Rather than an exhaustive list of every possible API call, this guide focuses on the most useful and commonly executed operations for managing identity, compute, storage, networking, and monitoring in Azure. Each API example includes the HTTP method, endpoint, required headers, sample payloads, and equivalent CLI/PowerShell commands for quick reference.

Authentication Overview

BEFORE MAKING ANY REST API calls, you must authenticate using Azure Active Directory and acquire an access token.

Get Access Token via Azure CLI

AZ ACCOUNT GET-ACCESS-token—resource https://management.azure.com

Access Token Response

{

"accessToken": "eyJ0eXAiOiJKV1QiLCJub25jZSI6...",

"expiresOn": "2025-01-01 12:00:00.000000",

"subscription": "xxxx-xxxx-xxxx-xxxx",

"tenant": "xxxx-xxxx-xxxx-xxxx",

"tokenType": "Bearer"

}

Use the accessToken in the Authorization header for all requests:

Authorization: Bearer <accessToken>

Subscription and Resource Group APIs

List All Subscriptions

GET HTTPS://MANAGEMENT.azure.com/subscriptions?api-version=2020-01-01

Create Resource Group

PUT HTTPS://MANAGEMENT.azure.com/subscriptions/{subscriptionId}/resourcegroups/{resourceGroupName}?api-v

Body:

{

"location": "uksouth",

"tags": {

"Environment": "Test"

}

}

Equivalent CLI:

az group create—name rg-example—location uksouth

Virtual Machines

Create VM (Simplified Example)

PUT HTTPS://MANAGEMENT.azure.com/subscriptions/{subscriptionId}/resourceGroups/{rg}/providers/Microsoft.Compute/virtualMachines/{vmName}?api-version=2023-03-01

Body:

```
{
"location": "uksouth",
"properties": {
"hardwareProfile": {
"vmSize": "Standard_B1s"
},
"osProfile": {
"computerName": "vmName",
"adminUsername": "azureuser",
"adminPassword": "YourP@ssword123"
},
"storageProfile": {
"imageReference": {
"publisher": "Canonical",
```

```
"offer": "UbuntuServer",

"sku": "18.04-LTS",

"version": "latest"

},

"osDisk": {

"createOption": "FromImage"

}

},

"networkProfile": {

"networkInterfaces": [

{

"id":
"/subscriptions/{subscriptionId}/resourceGroups/{rg}/providers/
Microsoft.Network/networkInterfaces/{nicName}"

}

]

}

}

}
```

Start/Stop/Delete VM

POST HTTPS://MANAGEMENT.azure.com/subscriptions/{subId}/resourceGroups/{rg}/providers/Microsoft.Compute/virtualMachines/{vmName}/start?api-version=2023-03-01

POST https://.../deallocate?api-version=...

DELETE https://.../virtualMachines/{vmName}?api-version=...

CLI Equivalents:

az vm start—name vmName—resource-group rg

az vm stop—name vmName—resource-group rg

az vm delete—name vmName—resource-group rg—yes

Storage Accounts

Create Storage Account

PUT HTTPS://MANAGEMENT.azure.com/subscriptions/{subscriptionId}/resourceGroups/{rg}/providers/Microsoft.Storage/storageAccounts/{accountName}?api-version=2023-01-01

Body:

{

"location": "uksouth",

"sku": {

"name": "Standard_LRS"

},

"kind": "StorageV2",

"properties": {

"supportsHttpsTrafficOnly": true

}

}

CLI:

az storage account create—name mystorageacct—resource-group rg—location uksouth—sku Standard_LRS

Networking

Create Virtual Network

PUT HTTPS://MANAGEMENT.azure.com/subscriptions/{subscriptionId}/resourceGroups/{rg}/providers/Microsoft.Network/virtualNetworks/vnetName?api-version=2022-07-01

Body:

{

"location": "uksouth",

"properties": {

"addressSpace": {

"addressPrefixes": ["10.0.0.0/16"]

},

"subnets": [

{

"name": "default",

"properties": {

"addressPrefix": "10.0.1.0/24"

}

}

]

}

}

NSG Rules

PUT HTTPS://MANAGEMENT.azure.com/subscriptions/{subscriptionId}/resourceGroups/{rg}/providers/Microsoft.Network/networkSecurityGroups/myNSG/securityRules/AllowSSH?api-version=2022-05-01

Body:

{

"properties": {

"protocol": "Tcp",

"sourcePortRange": "*",

"destinationPortRange": "22",

"sourceAddressPrefix": "*",

"destinationAddressPrefix": "*",

"access": "Allow",

"priority": 100,

"direction": "Inbound"

}

}

Monitoring and Alerts

Create Metric Alert

PUT HTTPS://MANAGEMENT.azure.com/subscriptions/{subId}/resourceGroups/{rg}/providers/microsoft.insights/metricAlerts/HighCPU?api-version=2021-09-01

Body:

{

"location": "global",

"tags": {},

"properties": {

"description": "Alert when CPU > 80%",

```
"severity": 2,

"enabled": true,

"scopes": [

"/subscriptions/{subId}/resourceGroups/{rg}/providers/
Microsoft.Compute/virtualMachines/vmName"

],

"evaluationFrequency": "PT1M",

"windowSize": "PT5M",

"criteria": {

"odata.type":
"Microsoft.Azure.Monitor.MultipleResourceMultipleMetricCriteria",

"allOf": [

{

"name": "HighCPU",

"metricName": "Percentage CPU",

"metricNamespace": "Microsoft.Compute/virtualMachines",

"operator": "GreaterThan",

"threshold": 80,

"timeAggregation": "Average"

}

]
```

```
},
"autoMitigate": true,
"actions": []
}
}
```

Policy and Governance

Create and Assign Policy Definition

PUT HTTPS://MANAGEMENT.azure.com/subscriptions/{subId}/providers/Microsoft.Authorization/policyDefinitions/requireTagEnv?api-version=2021-06-01

Body:

```
{
"properties": {
"displayName": "Require Environment tag",
"policyType": "Custom",
"mode": "All",
"parameters": {
"tagName": {
"type": "String",
"metadata": {
```

"displayName": "Tag Name",

"description": "Name of the tag"

}

}

},

"policyRule": {

"if": {

"field": "[parameters('tagName')]",

"exists": "false"

},

"then": {

"effect": "deny"

}

}

}

}

Assign the policy:

PUT https://management.azure.com/subscriptions/{subId}/resourceGroups/{rg}/providers/Microsoft.Authorization/policyAssignments/requireTagAssignment?api-version=2021-06-01

Body:

```
{
"properties": {
"displayName": "Enforce Environment Tag",
"policyDefinitionId": "/subscriptions/{subId}/providers/Microsoft.Authorization/policyDefinitions/requireTagEnv",
"parameters": {
"tagName": {
"value": "Environment"
}
}
}
}
```

SDK References

AZURE OFFERS OFFICIAL SDKs in several programming languages:

- **.NET SDK**:https://github.com/Azure/azure-sdk-for-net
- **Python SDK**:https://github.com/Azure/azure-sdk-for-python
- **Java SDK**:https://github.com/Azure/azure-sdk-for-java

- **JavaScript/TypeScript SDK**:https://github.com/Azure/azure-sdk-for-js

All SDKs support identity authentication, logging, and support for long-running operations via polling mechanisms.

Final Recommendations

- Use **Postman** or **Insomnia** for testing raw Azure REST API calls.
- Automate repetitive tasks with **Azure CLI**, **PowerShell**, or **Terraform**.
- Referencehttps://learn.microsoft.com/en-us/rest/api/azure/ for the complete and updated API documentation.

BY COMBINING API ACCESS with infrastructure automation and scripting, Azure Administrators can scale operational efficiency, enforce compliance, and build reliable cloud environments that align with organizational goals and cloud-native principles.

Frequently Asked Questions

THIS SECTION CONSOLIDATES some of the most commonly asked questions by candidates preparing for the AZ-104 Microsoft Azure Administrator certification, along with insights relevant to practicing administrators in real-world environments. These FAQs cover topics including exam logistics, Azure best practices, troubleshooting, governance, automation, cost management, and post-certification development.

Whether you're preparing for the exam, administering live environments, or aiming for career advancement, these answers serve as a rapid-access reference.

Exam and Certification

Q: HOW LONG IS THE AZ-104 exam, and how many questions should I expect?

The exam duration is approximately 150 minutes, and you can expect between 40 to 60 questions. These may include multiple-choice, drag-and-drop, case studies, and hot area questions.

Q: Is the AZ-104 exam open book?

No. You are not permitted to consult notes, web browsers, or external documentation during the exam, even if taken from home.

Q: What is the passing score for AZ-104?

700 out of 1000 is the passing threshold. Scores are scaled, not raw counts of correct answers.

Q: How long is the AZ-104 certification valid?

Once passed, the certification is valid for **1 year**, but can be renewed **for free** via Microsoft Learn by completing a short online assessment.

Q: Can I take the AZ-104 exam at home?

Yes. Microsoft offers both in-person and online proctored options. For online exams, ensure a quiet, isolated environment and pass the system check in advance.

Identity and Access Management

Q: WHAT'S THE DIFFERENCE between Azure AD roles and Azure RBAC?

- **Azure AD roles** manage directory-level actions like user creation and MFA configuration.
- **Azure RBAC** controls access to Azure resources like VMs, Storage, etc.

Q: What are the best practices for assigning permissions?

- Assign roles at the **lowest possible scope** (resource or resource group).
- Use **built-in roles** unless there's a strict need for a custom role.
- Prefer assigning **groups** over individual users to simplify management.

Q: Can I use Azure AD to protect Linux VMs?

Yes, by enabling **Azure AD login** for Linux and installing the extension. It's common in RBAC-based access scenarios for SSH.

Resource and Cost Management

Q: HOW DO I ENSURE that developers don't leave expensive resources running?

- Set **budgets** and configure alerting in **Cost Management.**
- Use **Azure Policies** to restrict VM sizes.

- Implement **automation runbooks** to shut down idle VMs during non-business hours.

Q: How can I track spending per team or environment?

Use **resource tags** like Team=DevOps or Environment=Production and review them in Cost Analysis with grouping filters.

Q: What services are eligible for Azure free tier?

Common free services include:

- 750 hours/month of B1S VMs (12 months)
- 250 GB of SQL Database (12 months)
- Always-free options like Azure Functions, Event Grid, and App Services (limited tier)

Q: What's the difference between budget alerts and spending limits?

- **Budget alerts** notify stakeholders but do **not** enforce any action.
- **Spending limits** (available on certain account types) **stop** deployments when reached.

Networking and Security

Q: WHEN SHOULD I USE Azure Firewall over NSGs?

- **NSGs** operate at Layer 4 (TCP/UDP) and are resource-level.

- **Azure Firewall** provides stateful inspection, Layer 7 filtering, threat intelligence, and logging across subnets.

Q: Can I assign public IPs to multiple VMs?

Each public IP must be bound to a specific NIC. You can use **Azure Load Balancer** or **Application Gateway** to share a public IP across multiple VMs.

Q: What's the recommended way to restrict access to Azure Storage?

- Enable **Private Endpoints.**
- Use **Shared Access Signatures (SAS)** with expiration.
- Deny public access and use **Azure AD authentication** for granular control.

Automation and Monitoring

Q: HOW DO I AUTOMATE resource deployment in Azure?

Common methods include:

- **Bicep** (Microsoft's ARM DSL)
- **Terraform** (cross-cloud, open-source)
- **Azure CLI/Powershell scripts**
- Use **Azure DevOps** or **GitHub Actions** for CI/CD pipelines

Q: What's the difference between Log Analytics and Azure Monitor?

- **Azure Monitor** is the overarching platform.
- **Log Analytics** is the workspace backend where telemetry and logs are stored.
- You use **KQL** to query the data in Log Analytics.

Q: How can I set up automatic actions from alerts?

Configure an **Action Group** that triggers:

- Email/SMS/Webhook
- Azure Function
- Logic App
- ITSM connector

Governance and Compliance

Q: WHAT'S THE BEST way to enforce tagging policies?

Use **Azure Policy** with a "modify" effect to automatically append missing tags or "deny" effect to block non-compliant resources.

Q: How do I restrict which regions resources can be deployed into?

Create a policy that evaluates the location field and denies resources deployed outside of approved regions.

Q: How can I detect non-compliant resources?

- Use **Azure Policy assignments** and view compliance state.
- Run **Azure Resource Graph** queries across subscriptions.
- Export policy evaluations to Log Analytics for long-term tracking.

Real-World Operations

Q: HOW CAN I CHECK effective permissions for a user?

Use:

az role assignment list—assignee user@domain.com

Or check via the Azure Portal > Access Control (IAM) > Check access.

Q: My VM won't start. What should I check?

- Quotas (especially for region-specific vCPUs)
- NSG rules blocking RDP/SSH
- Storage account or disk corruption
- Review **boot diagnostics** and **activity logs**

Q: How do I recover deleted resources?

- VMs: Restore from **backup** or **snapshot**

- Key Vault secrets: Use **soft delete and purge protection**
- Blobs: Enable **soft delete for blob storage**

Career and Learning

Q: WHAT CERTIFICATION should I take after AZ-104?

Depends on your goal:

- **AZ-305**: Solutions Architect
- **AZ-500**: Security Engineer
- **AZ-400**: DevOps Engineer
- **DP-203**: Data Engineer
- **SC-300**: Identity and Access Administrator

Q: How do I get practical experience without production access?

- Use a **free-tier account** or create a sandbox in **Microsoft Learn**
- Deploy in Dev/Test subscriptions with low-cost resources
- Contribute to open-source projects that use Azure (GitHub)

Q: How do I stay updated?

- Followhttps://azure.microsoft.com/updates

- Join the **Microsoft Tech Community**
- Read **Azure Weekly**, watch **John Savill's YouTube** channel, and engage in **LinkedIn/Reddit communities**

Miscellaneous

Q: WHAT'S THE DIFFERENCE between ARM and Bicep?

- **ARM templates** use JSON and are verbose.
- **Bicep** is a cleaner, more readable DSL that compiles to ARM.
- Both are supported and integrated into Azure natively.

Q: What services are included in Azure Advisor recommendations?

- Cost
- Performance
- Availability
- Security
- Operational excellence

Q: Can I move resources between subscriptions or regions?

Yes, but with caveats. Some services (e.g., VMs with public IPs, VNets) have region lock-in and require re-creation. Always reviewmove support matrix[18].

Summary

THESE FAQS REFLECT the most pressing and recurring questions asked by both exam candidates and working Azure administrators. Bookmark this section as a rapid troubleshooting and policy reference. Continually revisit it as Azure evolves and new practices, constraints, and automation patterns emerge. Confidence in Azure administration comes not just from knowledge, but from experience solving real-world challenges—and knowing where to look when questions arise.

---

18. https://learn.microsoft.com/en-us/azure/azure-resource-manager/management/move-support-resources

www.ingramcontent.com/pod-product-compliance
Lightning Source LLC
LaVergne TN
LVHW090259210926
848480LV00001B/76